U2 FARAWAY SO CLOSE

IT'S A **CELEBRATION** and it's an

adventure, the story of being with people that

you **LOVE** and having little side

VOYAGES into other territories.

And there are joys and there's

HAPPINESS and **PAIN**

and discovery and many many new people along the

way who you don't find but who find you. And it's

magic and it's **ROCK 'N'**

ROLL and the bottom line is love.

Yo **BABY !**

Welcome.

FREE YOUR MIND and your ass will

follow. The kingdom of heaven is within.

RAMALAMA, pussycats.

"Life is what happens to you when you're busy making other plans"
John Lennon

U2 FARAWAY SO CLOSE

Words & photographs by
BP Fallon

Design and art direction by
Steve Averill & Works Associates

Little, Brown and Company
BOSTON NEW YORK TORONTO LONDON

Bono and Edge and Larry ... oh, and Adam too ... they're walking ... well splashing actually ... splashing across Times Square NYC and it's the wee small hours of the morning and it's pissing down. It's the same old story, *another* video shoot with U2 in the cold: 'Gloria', 'Red Rocks,' 'Unforgettable Fire' and *even* for the 'Joshua Tree' desert shots the guys were freezing their arses off because the desert's fucking cold in winter. Always the cold.

And here we are in NYC and again and again they walk across Times Square, from under the Coca-Cola sign across towards the gigantic Sony video screen. They're soaked through, and Adam's not into it. He looks pissed off. Lord, you can't blame him.

Each time the band, who kinda look like The Beatles sploshing through Hamburg in some John Cassavetes movie ... Each time they reach the umbrella at their shivering destination they're touched up with towels, encouraged. Bono and Edge try to vibe Adam up, but he's feeling grouchy. "I mean, this isn't meant to be the bloody Monkees, is it?" is the vibe you're getting from Adam.

Phil Joanou bellows through a hi-tech low-fi megaphone each time the quartet splatters towards him, attempting to animate his video stars as knee-bent cameramen walk backwards filming their rock group. There's a pause in the proceedings and Bono spots the conspicuously conspicuous undercover cops hanging around outside McDonalds chomping on Big Macs and he borrows Phil's megaphone. "OK cops" Bono roars at them, "put down your French fries and come out with your hands up!" Next Bono borrows a mobile phone and calls Ali in Dublin, the rain pouring off his bedraggled head. "Good morning Ireland, how are ya? Ali: this is your wakeup call, how are my three babes doin' this morning?"

Bono, he's gotten on the *worst* patch leather platform boots. Not even kitsch enough to be cool. You tell him. "I guess," says Bono putting on his little boy look, "they aren't even *bad* enough to be good. They're shite, aren't they?".

Each time they make their determined stroll towards the umbrella, Bono, Edge, Larry and Adam keep walking across this large grille in the pavement.

"Look!" says Regine grabbing your arm. "Look! Did you see that?" "Uh? *Look?*" "There, coming out of the grille ...!" You look at the grille in the pavement and see a grille in the pavement. Shit, they have 'em all over the world ... even in Dublin. "Keep looking" instructs Regine. "I just saw a mouse pop its head up" she says, "keep looking carefully." Nothing happens. The guys rattle over the grille a few more times. Ah, Regine, c'mon. And then - sho' nuff, a little ol' New York mouse looks out, sniffs the damp air, and scuttles over to a long coffin-shaped box beside the railings by the road.

Behind these railings, parked there, is a New York police car with two of NY's finest observing the scene.

More mice pitter patter out of the pavement grille over to the box, into which they disappear. Someone says there aren't any mice in New York, just rats. The rats, they've eaten all the mice, someone else adds.

So, hell, these are *rats* right here in what is supposedly the middle of the so called civilised world. Here we are in Times Square and they're running all over the damned place. Rats!

Phil is filming and the four lads keep splashing back and forth ... U2 wading through the puddles all in the name of making a video for 'One' ... this is megaworld success, huh?

And then Regine points to the box. She doesn't say anything, just points. As you leave her eyes to follow her gaze, you see that her face looks very very sad, heartbroken. Silently, she's pointing to the damp cardboard coffin-shaped box. Through the rain you see what she sees. There are two shoes visible at this end, the soles of two shoes. One sole, it moves, twitches. Then both of them. From the other end of the box some rats lethargically amble back to the grille, temporarily vanishing into the sewers of the world.

The top of the box opens and a man staggers to his feet, his hands scratching his face. He shakes his head a few times. He sees no one, nothing. The man, he lies down again among the rats and covers himself and his house guests with the cardboard lid of their home.

U2 begin another walk towards the cameras. The cops, they sit in their car, looking bored.

HERBERT, BRIGID MOONEY, CECILIA COFFEY, CILI
... GER WATTERS, PRINCIPLE MANAGEMENT INC
TV SHOW ...
STS (PHILIPS VIDIWALL, DIGIWALL AND MONITOR IN
WORK, MARK PELLINGTON, PETER "WILLIE" WILLIAI
OWENS, EXECUTIVE PRODUCER VIDIWALL AND DI

Dramatis

PERSONAE

EXECUTIVE PRODUCER

The Manager

Sheila

Holly

Sharon

Suzanne

Sheila

Eileen

Yer man

Cristina

Regine

February 24th 1992, Civic Center Production Rehearsals

Heck, there's a helluva lot of people on this tour. Here at Lakeland in Florida there's this Irish band and Paul McGuinness who's their manager ...

Paul's PA is Sheila Roche, who you first met *years ago* backstage at the ZZ Top concert at the SFX Hall in Dublin, Sheila this little punkette with Adam. You were there with Patsy. Phil Lynott, bless him, was vibing around too, still high on playing with Thin Lizzy in Texas with ZZ

Top. And now Sheila's the complete management associate, making everything more presentable so Paul can tackle it more easily and looking sharper than her boss in her own pinstriped suit.

Moptop hair, glasses and so warm you could make toast off her, Ellen Darst used to work for Warners Records and fell in love with U2 when they first appeared in America, saying to Paul "I'd love to work with you when you can afford me." Now she's Director of the Principle

Management office in New York. Holly Peters, like Sheila born in Dublin and working out of the New York office, is Ellen's PA on the tour, one of the most rock'n'roll people in the world-beating management team which Paul McGuinness has put together.

Dennis Sheehan clucks around like a strict yet kindly mother hen who makes certain none of the chicklets stray or get out of line.

Dennis, he's the punctilious and precise soft-spoken Tour Manager. Well before you're on the plane to America you have in your hands the Zoo TV tour itinerary book, an extraordinary and brilliant piece of work so detailed that it tells you exactly what time you're supposed to be leaving your hotel in Portland Oregon three months down the line. Dennis, he used to work for Led Zeppelin, coming into the organization to assist Zeppo's tour manager Richard Cole. You first met him at Chicago airport twenty years ago when he was detailed to pick you

hingy

Anne-Louise

Morleigh

Maurice

up from a flight from London to join Zeppelin in the Windy City. This last insignificant piece of information is only remembered by you when you're halfway through Europe. "Did you once pick me up in Chicago, Dennis?" you ask. "Yes" he says, and it all floods back to you: this impeccably polite gentleman pointing out the tallest building in the world and probably thinking his passenger was *weird*. That was then. Or was it?

Regine is the lady who first pointed you out to Bono, as Bono tells it. Bono was at The Ramones concert at the Phibsboro Grand in Dublin in 1978 and asked her who was the guy in the green velvet dressing-gown. You originally met Regine through her brother Johnnie Fingers when you worked with him and Geldof as paid mouth for

The Boomtown Rats. Like Johnnie, Regine played keyboards, playing in the Dublin group The New Versions. After joining Island Records to work in the press office, U2 "borrowed" her to work with them on an Australian tour and later she set up her own PR company RMP with U2 as her first clients. Now Regine travels with U2 as their highly lauded press co-ordinator, often joined by Sharon Blankson who used to work with Frank Murray

HOMBRES

Nassim, natch!

Yer man again

when Frank managed The Pogues. Regine and Sharon's job is bloody hard, fielding lunatics while keeping everybody sweet. Actually, *everybody* on the U2 team works bloody hard. One of Paul McGuinness's many skills is in discovering bright and talented people, and getting them to work their arses off on behalf of not only the group but themselves.

Suzanne Doyle, shining light under the weight of unrelentless logistics, is the most hugging and huggable person on the tour. Suzanne, she's an *angel* - a tough angel if necessary mind ya, the Assistant Tour Manager with a clipboard in her hand and a portable phone to her ear, with the most **draining** job of anyone and **loved** by everybody. Suzanne, during the 'Lovetown' tour, she worked with U2 doing ticketing, sorting out guest lists and passes for blaggers and journalists and VIPs alike. After going to Australia where she worked for an indie record label, Suzanne joined the Zoo TV tour in arguably the most stressful job for any mere mortal. No, most **everyone's** job could be stressful as hell. Fun too, mind you, buckets of fun. And Suzanne, after corralling the troops, "bags ready at 11.30 and down in the lobby at 1 o'clock", making sure we get to wherever on time, with Dennis miraculously finding an extra jet or two if necessary, herding us into the

smoker, he's kind and tolerant and will forever dole out large wallops of money to you as long as you sign your name on a bit of paper. "Don't spend more than you're earning" is his continual paternal wisdom. Lovely people, he and his wife Gretchen. Should've taken his advice ...

Fintan Fitzgerald changed the face of Zoo TV. It was he who found the original Fly shades in a secondhand shop and gave them to Bono as a present. "It's Fighting Fintan Fitzgerald's job to make sure that we don't look like wankers or if we do, it's by our own design" as Bono so succinctly puts it. Shaven-headed Fintan, he's Head Of Wardrobe, with always the hottest new sounds pumping from his ghetto blaster. Assisting Fintan in the styling department are Nassim Khalifa whose speciality is

Fintan

Dan

Suzanne aris

mo' Sheila

Kerun

Holly une fois encore

transport in the encore during 'Desire' if we're doing a runner from the gig and ticking our names off and congratulating you if you're on time, ensuring that everyone from Robert De Niro and Julia Roberts to Brendan Bowyer and Axl Rose are treated royally, she is always the first to party hearty. Shit, she sure deserves it after some of us have driven her mad! Thank God for Suzanne.

Dan Russell, who runs a recording studio in Los Angeles and is very buddy buddy with T Bone Burnett, now does ticketing often aided by his chum Harold Hallas.

Bob Koch is the man with the money, the Tour Business Manager from Media, PA. A born again non-

whacking on makeup with the skill of a plastic surgeon, transforming monsters into semi human beings, and Helen Campbell who unknowingly has the unfortunate task ahead of her of sewing together your Son Of Sam suit *as well* as looking after some ol' rock group from Ireland. Thanx, Helen. One night in Hamburg you t h i n k you're seeing Nassim on MTV in a Depeche Mode video. Ah, dreams. In one eye and out the other till you see the evidence on a contact sheet.

"We seem to have a lot of women working for us" Bono will observe blithely, "but in fact I think it's the other way around!"

On the move, most everything is videoed. The producer of Zoo TV is Ned O'Hanlon, he and his director Maurice Linnane shadowing the group everywhere abetted by the camera work of Gerry MacArthur and Richard Kendrick on sound. Brilliant, these cats, often working through the night for days on end, whizzing to editing studios in the nearest part of the world and returning to the Zoo with something really fine under their arms.

Jerry Mele is Chief Of Security, a Vietnam vet who came back from the tortured hell of search and destroy to cold turkey from junk by tying himself to his bed. A fantastic man, gentle, humble. To observe him instructing the local security at every gig is a truly heart-warming experience. He tells the local muscle to take it easy, to remember that the reason they're there, the reason we're *all* here, is "for the kids". The way Jerry tells it, it isn't corny. Darrell

Sharon vair amháin eile

TOY

Ellen

Lyndsey

Dennis

Ives has Bono as his main responsibility, while David Guyer will often hit the highway with Larry on his Harley. Tim Ross, moustache and still with the echo of his military background, is the tricky one. At first you don't like each other but he chills out, suggests you say "Time out" when it's getting uncomfortable. He talks about his job in the army guarding generals and upper brass, how, thank God, it never got wet - a euphemism for blood being spilt. From underneath his gruff exterior emerges a warm and genial individual. Jerry from Phoenix, Darrell and Tim from Detroit, David from Los Angeles: a great team. Jerry ... or Darrell or Tim or David ... go up to the fans waiting outside of the gigs or outside of the hotels and ask them to stand back, that the band will go up to them and that these fans, they'll get their autographs if they don't freak out.

In the end as in the beginning, without the fans none of this would exist.

Zoology Then & Now Sometimes: BONO THE EDGE ADAM CLAYTON LARRY MULLEN JNR PAUL MCGUINNESS Manager. Principle Management Ltd (Dublin): ANNE-LOUISE KELLY Director BARBARA GALAVAN JACKIE BENNETT EILEEN LONG DAVID HERBERT MARIE DUFFY BRIGID MOONEY CECILIA COFFEY CILLIAN GUIDERA LIZ DEVLIN ANNE O'LEARY CANDIDA BOTTACI SANDRA LONG. Principle Management Inc. (New York): ELLEN DARST Director KERYN KAPLAN Director SHEILA ROCHE BESS DULANEY NIKKI DE GIOIA & DEE SUSIE SMITH. Tour Personnel: DENNIS SHEEHAN Tour Manager BOB KOCH Tour Accountant SHEILA ROCHE Management Associate REGINE MOYLETT Press Co-ordinator SHARON BLANKSON Mo' Press Co-ordinating DAN RUSSELL & HAROLD HALLIS Ticketing BP FALLON Guru Viber And Disc Jockey PATSY DENNEHY King Boogaloo Cloak DONAL MOYLAN/HELEN CAMPBELL/EDGE Son Of Sam II Suit VAUGHN MARTINIAN Boogaloo Ghettoblaster Transport SUZANNE DOYLE Assistant to Dennis Sheehan HOLLY PETERS Assistant to Ellen Darst FINTAN FITZGERALD Head Of Wardrobe NASSIM KHALIFA Wardrobe/Makeup HELEN CAMPBELL Wardrobe/Stylist JERRY MELE Security Chief. TIM ROSS Security & Luggage. Security: DARREL IVES DAVID GRYER ERIC HAUSCH SCOTT NICHOLS. CHRISTINA PETRO Dancer MORLEIGH STEINBERG Choreographer & Dancer. Gorilla Video & Dreamchaser Vibes: NED O'HANLON Producer MAURICE LINNANE Director GERRY MACARTHUR Cameraman RICHARD KENDRICK Sound. STEVE IREDALE Production Manager JOE O'HERLIHY House Sound Engineer JOHN "JAKE" KENNEDY Deputy Production Manager TIM BUCKLEY Production Co-Ordinator PETER "WILLIE" WILLIAMS Production Designer/Head Of Taste TIM LAMB Stage Manager ROCCO REEDY Assistant Stage Manager RICK TAYLOR Production Accountant PAULETTE GARNEAU Tour Accountant DAVID HERBERT Production Secretary ROBBIE ADAMS Effects Engineer DAVE CLAYTON Keyboard Programming DES BROADBERY Keyboard Technician SAM O'SULLIVAN Drum Technician FRASER MCALISTER Guitar Technician DALLAS SCHOO Guitar Technician STUART MORGAN Bass Technician & Australia COLM "RAB" MCALLISTER Tour Technician RICHARD HARTMAN Production Engineer DRAGAN KUZMANOV Head Carpenter ADAM "AJ" RANKIN Carpenter JAN PAULSEN Carpenter ADELE HOCKING Carpenter/Silver Trabbie Viber CHARLIE BOXHALL Head Rigger TJ THOMPSON Chief Rigger. Riggers: WARREN JONES PETE KALAPSIDIOTIS MARK "SMOKIE" KOHORN. JOE RAVITCH PA Crew Chief CJ PATTERSON Chief Stage Technician STEVE MCCALE Monitor Technician/MC to King Boogaloo BILLY LOUTHE PA Technician/Electrician/Servicing The Silver Machine SCOTT APPLETON On Stage Microphone Man/MC to Son Of Sam II DAVE SKAFF Monitor Technician DON GARBER PA Technician KEVIN SHIRLEY Lighting Crew Chief SIMON CARUS - WILSON Colourmag Operator RUSSEL "BITS" LYONS Lighting Technician FIRMIN MORIARTY Lighting Technician RICK ANDERSON Lighting Technician MATT PATERSON Lighting Technician SEAN FOWLER Lighting Technician CAROL DODDS Live Video Director BOB LONEY Chief Video Engineer/Projection JOHN DAVID WILLIAMS Video Projectionist RICHARD DAVIS Vidiwall Projection DAVE LEMMINK Video Engineer DAVE NEUGEBUER Assistant Video Engineer MONICA CASTON Assistant Director BRUCE RAMOS Camera Operator 1 LISA LONEY Camera Operator 2 MIKE TRIBBLE Handheld Camera CHRIS PARKES Merchandising Management JEREMY JOSEPH Winterland Productions JOHN PANARO Merchandising Supervisor DAN PANARO KEVIN WEGMAN Merchandising. Flying Saucers Catering: HELEN FINDLEY DENISE "DEE" EDWARDS ROBERT GRANTHAM-WISE JODI BRAKE TINA "FELIX" MAKIN MARY CAIRD ELIZABETH ADSHEAD LINDA AUGUSTINE NEDRA BALDORI DUGGIE & SUZANNE Vagabond: SETH NETTLES Island: CB & MARY Island (Dublin) DAVE PENNEFATHER CAROLINE SANDRA JOHN O'REILLY Island (London) PHIL COOPER Island (NY) PEGGY DOLD Polygram (US) RICK DOBBIS & MARIANNE KOENIG JOHN BARBIS JEFF JONES DENNIS FINE SKY DANIELS STEVE LEEDS, REBECCA HOWARD PARR, VONETTE JOERICCITELLE NANCY SULLIVAN SUSAN CLARY GLORIA BOYCE AMY FERGUSON. Video Staging Concept by BRIAN ENO Philips Vidiwall and Moniter Images by BRIAN ENO MARK PELLINGTON PETER WILLIAMS Coordination by NED O'HANLON ("Yo, Ned!") PETER "WILLIE" WILLIAMS Trabant Lighting. Trabant Design: CATHERINE OWENS RENE CASTRO Trabant Engineering: WARREN STEADMAN IAN WHITAKER. Professional Services: Premier Talent Agency New York FRANK BARSALONA BARBARA SKYDEL Wasted Talent Agency London IAN FLOOKS OJ Kilkenny & Co Accounts Dublin OSSIE KILKENNY BRIAN MURPHY ALAN DUFFY ALAN MCEVOY FRANCES BRENNAN COLETTE ROONEY DELORES FERRIS OJK & Co Accounts London PAT SAVAGE Robbins Speilman Slayton & Co. Accountants New York BRUCE SLAYTON SHELLEY MESSINGER Meibach Epstein Reiss & Regis Lawyers New York INA MEIBACH GEORGE REGIS BARRY REISS Bridge Wolsey Solicitors (London) JAMES WOLSEY AMANDA HARCOURT Winterland Productions Merchandising Production and Servicing (USA): DEL FURANO Publicity: Wasserman Group Inc. Los Angeles PAUL WASSERMAN BRIAN O'NEAL RMP Publicity London REGINE MOYLETT SHARON BLANKSON Ferret & Spanner Ltd Radio & TV PR (UK) NIGEL SWEENEY Tour Services: Clair Bros Audio (USA) Troy Clair Light and Sound Design Inc (USA) John Lobell Light and Sound Design Ltd (Set Construction UK) Terry Lee Nocturne Productions Inc (Video) (USA) Pat Morrow Upstaging Inc (Trucking) (USA) Robin Shaw Barry Slattery Insurance Brokers Ltd (Dublin) BARRY SLATTERY Robertson Taylor Insurance Brokers (London New York) WILLIE ROBERTSON BOB TAYLOR Tait Towers Set Construction (USA) MICHAEL TAIT Fox Info Systems (USA) DAVID COOPER BILL BULLOCK Transportation: Arts & Entertainment Travel (USA) THERESA PESCO & BRET ALEXANDER Four Seasons Leasing Inc (USA) MIKE SLARVE Rock-It Cargo (UK) ALAN ESCOMBE BOB BROWN Rock-It Cargo (USA) DAVID BERNSTEIN KEVIN WADE & DIARMID Zoo TV Tour Programme written and edited by BP FALLON for BP Fallon Inc. Thanx To BARRY LAZELL Zooropa '93 foreword by BRIAN ENO Designed by STEVE AVERILL SHAUGHN MCGRATH BRIAN WILLIAMS ("Ramalama Pussycats! Thanx 4Ever") Works Associates (Dublin)

January 3rd 1992, Oakdown Road, Dublin

Bono's just been on the phone. He asked would you like to put together the tour programme, the book that they sell at the concerts, for U2's tour. "I mean, if you'd like to do it, if you have time. You could write it, or commission people to write it if you want." The band will be playing a lot of 'Achtung Baby' stuff. There's going to be loads of television screens, shooting out messages and visuals. Bono says it's going to be a travelling rock'n'roll TV station "beaming out across frontiers." It sounds pretty wild.

You said, yes, you'd love to do it. It's called 'Zoo TV'.

January 16th 1992, Dublin

We're in a tiny little room in The Factory. There's the band and Anne-Louise - Anne-Louise Kelly, the Director of Principle Management in Dublin - and you're showing them your work for the Zoo TV tour programme. Anne-Louise leaves the room and now there's only Bono, Edge, Adam and Larry. And you. And Bono pipes up "If we asked you, would you come on the road with us?" and you answer "If you asked me, I would". They never ask you but you go anyway.

January 27th 1992, Dublin

You're on the phone to Jackie Bennett at the office and she's saying "BP, we really have to have your credit for the tour programme *now*" and you're saying "Well I can't really put 'Guru, Viber and Discjockey', can I?" and Jackie's saying "Why not?" and thus it is.

'BP Fallon: Guru, Viber and Discjockey.' Yo baby!

February 1992, before tour, Dublin

You're headed down Merrion Square to the National Gallery to seek out the famous painting of Jesus in the crown of thorns done a couple of centuries ago by some superfamous Italian cat whose name you can't remember. You know, the picture of Jesus looking up in the air with his eyes almost on the nod, blood streaming down his face. In colour.

"Why do you want to see that?" Sinéad asks.

"Because I want to adapt it for the tour ..."

Sinéad blurts out caringly "Don't you think Bono's had enough of being God? Bono and Jesus! Bloody hell, Beep!"

The Beep plan is different, tho': Elvis in a crown of thorns, garish, vulgar, the crucified king, on the back of King Boogaloo's purple cape. Just want to check the original, baby.

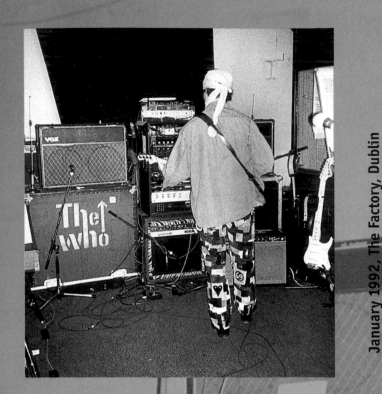

Ronnie Wood comes barrelling up the stairs of The Factory, vibey and grinning and laughing as usual, followed by his pal Bernard Fowler. Bernard, he sang backing vocals with The Stones on their Urban Jungle Steel Wheels extravaganza, sings with Ronnie on his non-Stone new album 'Slide On This'. Edge, too, he plays on Ron's album, went down to Ronnie's house in County Kildare and put down some guitar, joining other guests on the album like Hothouse Flowers and Joe Elliot from Def Leppard.

In the rehearsal room, Edge is playing through an old Vox amp atop a flight case that belonged to Pete Townsend many Keith Moons ago. The case, it still proudly bears the original Who logo, the Maximum R'n'B visual with the arrow built into the name.

Ronnie, he's taken a fancy to the skills of Edge's guitar tec Dallas, been trying to woo him off to work with Ron and The Stones. Prince, too, has been dangling carrots at Dallas. But Dallas, he's stickin' close to the Edge.

Ron, he's all loud grinnerama, the Jack the lad with the black pineapple haircut atop his head. Diamond.

U2, they're all industrious, more concentrated than a can of orange juice. You wonder does Ron expect to jam with them on 'Little Red Rooster' or 'Down The Road Apiece'. A couple of years ago walking into U2, they'd be well ready for a blast of twangerama. But right now the band have their screwdriver out and the noise that is coming out of the studio is cyber subterranean, fuckin' sci-fi. Ronnie and Bernard, they rapidly flash off the industrial work vibe and depart noisily like two schoolboys on the hop. Bono, too, splits shortly afterwards to visit a relative in hospital, then hustles back into the room scrambling for his car keys. The keys, they can't be found **anywhere**. Bono, he thrusts his hands into his sheepskin jacket, fumbles. "Oh, I had them all the time" he says.

Food is ordered. And shortly dinner arrives, steaming fish'n'chips from Burdocks. With this band it's either high life or low life and never the in-between. Yesterday it was caviar. Now Edge, Adam and Larry, they squat down on the floor and stuff chips into their gobs ...

"The pursuit of trivia, the search for soul. Something like that. I don't know what the fuck it's about. Looking for Jesus in a trashcan ..."

"Is that a line from a song?"

"No ... uh, but it might be"

Bono's on the phone, talking 'bout the new record U2 are making. In Dublin it's nine in the morning and he's up and about while where you find yourself, wide awake on Joe King Carrasco's Rancho No Tengo in the woods near Austin, Texas, it's three in the wee small hours.

Adam called a few days previously, vibing. "Are you still writing songs with Joe King? Well, we're doing some great work here. It's coming much easier than 'Achtung Baby'. We're having no problems with the music - the music is just comin' and y'know it's really down to whether Bono feels he's got enough time to get the lyrics to the place that he wants to get them. His starting points are good, it's just how long it's gonna take him to get happy with them ..."

And now Bono's on the blower bubbling, speeding and letting go of the wheel. No brakes even ...

You haven't seen him since four months before, at

It goes, let me see, what's the opening line: 'You don't know where you took it, you just know what you got' ... I'm just working on clues.

"'Wake Up Dead Man', instrumentally it's quite a Gothic piece, very powerful playing from Edge and I really love the bass on it.

"There's another song called 'Lemon', a throwaway groove but a great groove ... Adam is playing with a great deal of swagger and very very much in the pocket and on with Larry."

BP: "Adam was getting so funky during the tour, and Larry was playin' like Charlie Watts, crackin' like a whip".

Bono: "Adam, yeah, he's answering to the name of Sparky at the moment. There's even a song called 'Sparky's Left The Planet'."

And then Bono is elaborating on the song Johnny Cash has cut with U2. "You know we wrote it in a day because Johnny Cash was coming in to Dublin and we had this song provisionally titled 'Wanderlust' - which we figured would suit Johnny Cash - and we thought if we're ever going to get Johnny Cash to sing it, this is the time."

"Y'know", says Bono, his mind butterflying, "he's

April 1993, Dublin, Ireland

Christmas at Edge's house.

And now Bono's talking 'bout the new music U2 are making in Dublin and he's doing a rabbit on some of the tracks. "This song 'Babyface' you'll like it, it's sorta throwaway but not quite. 'Since you came into my life, I'm dressing sharper' is all I've got so far.

"This other one we're working on, 'Hold Me, Thrill Me, Kiss Me, Kill Me', it's about being in a rock'n'roll band I suppose, being a star, whatever that is.

such a big man and you can see Johnny Cash is where Elvis got a lot of his attitude ... Elvis would have been a cissy without Johnny Cash to hang out with. All that *attitude* ... that was Big John. Johnny, he was 'de man'." Next thing we're talking about Johnny Cash driving Bono around his zoo in Nashville, Bono relating "and Johnny was telling me that he had this llama - no, what's the big bird, an emu, yeah. He had this emu" and now Bono is telling you in his best Johnny Cash voice "'Bono, it almost

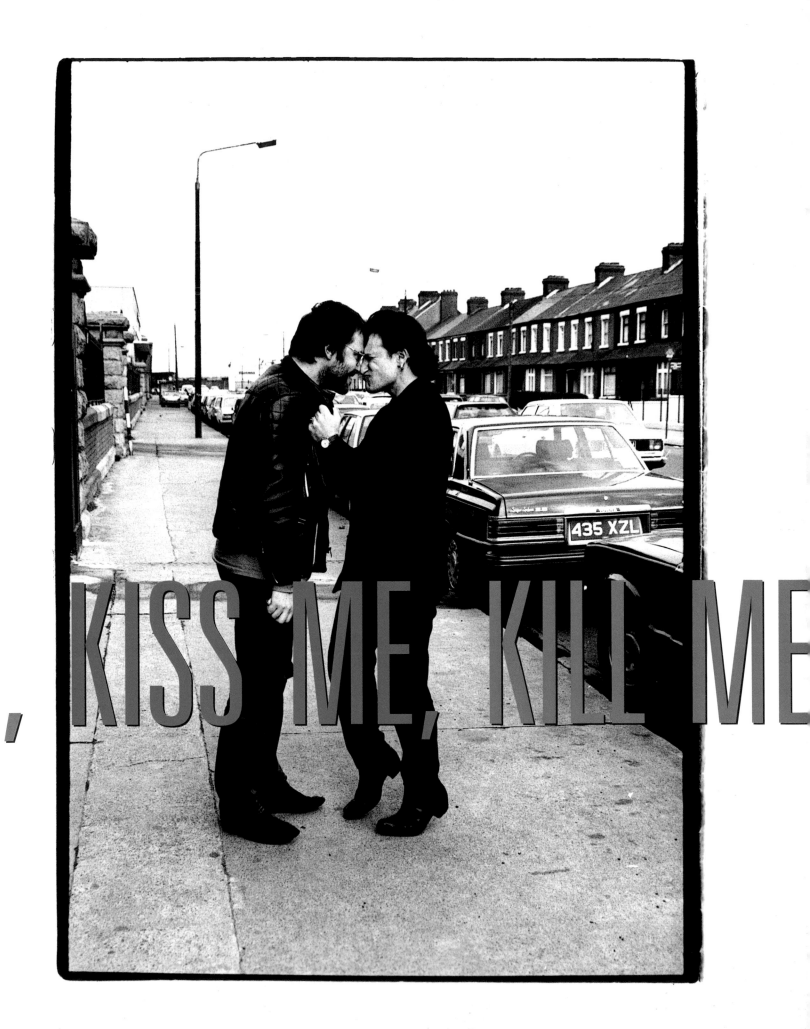

killed me. If I hadn't a stick in my hand I was a dead man.' It broke two of his ribs and tried to trample him to death, and all I could think of was 'Johnny Cash Killed By Emu'..."

We chuckle in awe of this averted catastrophe and, never mind that, in awe of this great man Johnny Cash. Even winners got scars, baby.

"Anyway, it goes like this", Bono says.

And for the next three minutes Telecom Eireann is broadcasting Bono singing, going "... where men can't walk and freely talk and men turn their fathers in, ah stopped outside a church-house where the citizens like to sit, they say they want the kingdom but they don't want God in it, yeah ah went wanderin', nothin' but the thought of you ...".

BP: "You said there's a sort of techno thing in it?"

Bono: "Yeah, but kitsch ... The Holiday Inn From Hell band!"

Bono, blast it, he's such a warm man and just talking to him all enthusiastic casts a spell. Dammit, this bastard is drawing you in, making you want to hear the music, making you want to face the music and see the eyes of the guys who are making it.

Of course you have to go, whether Sparky's left the planet or not. And of course you want to, because it moves you, makes you happy, this music and these people making it. So you ride the mystery plane and swap the Tex Mex sunshine for the drizzly damp of Dublin and go to The Factory in Barrow Street.

None of the band are around.

So you walk around the corner to Ringsend Road Studios where Bono is dressed in black and ensconced in a metal chair, his Johnny Cash lyrics spread over the mixing desk. To his left is Flood, whose latest production, Depeche Mode's 'Songs Of Faith And Devotion' album, has just entered the British charts at No. 1. "And it's No. 1 in America too, everywhere, even in Cavan" champions Bono.

Again and again Bono sings bits of the song, sometimes meshing with Johnny Cash's deep dark voice and other times gliding alongside it. More searching for clues, letting the muse channel him.

And now he's strolling back to The Factory, he and Flood, and in the Dublin rush-hour traffic the cars slow even more, slow to a fan's pace as windows are rolled down and speechless faces of all ages gawk excitedly until a little old lady in a Morris Minor sticks her head out and says "Simply the best." Bono grins "Do I really look like Tina Turner?"

In The Factory control room, Robbie is at the studio controls, Willie Mannion's doing tape op, Dallas crouches ever-ready and Flood plonks himself to the side

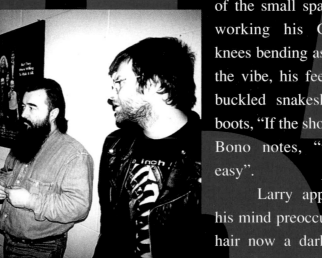

of the small space. Edge is working his Gretsch, his knees bending as he gets into the vibe, his feet encased in buckled snakeskin-patterned boots, "If the shoes are right", Bono notes, "the album's easy".

Larry appears briefly, his mind preoccupied and his hair now a darker shade of pale, then vanishes as quickly as he came.

Now Bono's singing a song provisionally titled 'Sinatra' - "I used to stay in to watch the adverts. I could lip sync the talk shows," then trying "I could lip sync the talk show host", then asking the room "What's better d'you think?" You notice a little darn about the size of an Irish

20p on the thigh of his faded black jeans.

Titles float around like confetti, like 'Last Night On Earth' and the crazed instrumental 'Nosejob'. Another song is called 'Untidy Life' and 'Daddy's Gonna Pay For Your Car Crash' has lyrics that go "dressed up like a car crash, leather and chrome ...", and then there's the poignant beauty of 'If God Will Send His Angels'.

Everything's changing. What'll end up on the finished record, God knows. And He ain't tellin', not yet. And none of the band know either.

Bono takes you into the Green Room to play you some tapes, fumbles for the song that he and Edge wrote for Al Green called 'Revolution Of The Heart' but can't find it. He pokes at the machine trusting some button will do something and whoosh! the speakers crackle with a sound like Madonna on helium. "That's strange", says Bono, prodding at the buttons some more. "Ah yeah" he figures as

the cassette settles into its normal speed, "it must have been set for fast dubbing ..."

He cracks in another cassette. "This is the first track where U2 ..." He pauses, grins, "where U2 sound like *men*." Suddenly 'Hold Me, Thrill Me, Kiss Me, Kill Me' explodes with vulgar ferocity, a below-the-belt dirty sound ... nah, a fucking *filthy* sound, raunch a go go. Shit, never mind *emus*. Bloody hell. This is rhinos in heat, horny as hell.

Now 'Wake Up Dead Man' is rushing from the speakers, Edge's guitar painting the sky and Adam's bass just powerful, powerful. Bono leans over and sings the as-yet-unrecorded vocals in your ear. "Jesus, Jesus help me, I'm alone in this world and a fucked up world it is too ... Jesus, I'm waiting here boss. I know you're looking out for us but maybe your hands aren't free. Your father who made the world in seven, He's in charge of heaven, could you put a word in for me ..." He leans away trembling. "So that's a very powerful piece and the lights in the console start going on and off. It's quite spooky ..."

At this precise point Adam crashes through the door like a cork from a champagne bottle, ricochets over to Bono and thrusts a wad of photos into his pal's hand, beaming. Taken at Adam's house by Anton Corbijn, they're shots of Adam and Naomi, tender and funky and loving. Then Adam yells "Listen to this, it's fucking amazing!" and dextrously whacks a CD into the machine. 3-D diddlied rap leaps at you like a sledgehammer blow to the back of the neck, perfect pumping power that'd crack nail varnish, Sinéad's voice also in the mix. "Marxmen, '33 Revolutions Per Minute', that's who it is " Adam extols. "Donal Lunny's son is in the group. Fucking amazing!" Adam's in his world, lost to the music. You've probably never seen a happier person in your life.

"I've heard people talking about having blanks, going through writer's block. I always remember when I was a kid, I remember being at school, when people were talking about Yeats, and how at this particular period in his life he couldn't write and he'd nothing he wanted to write and he was desperate about this. I remember I put up my hand and asked the teacher 'Well, I'm not trying to be smart or anything but why didn't he write about *that*?"

"I run away from writing words. Words are scary ..."

Bono

Another day ... Edge is seated in the corner of the control room at the Factory in an upright chair, figuring out a run on his Telecaster. Bono's ensconced in the squashy sofa with a typewriter computer thingy on his knees. "Can you work that?" you ask King B, this man in the middle of the matrix of Zoo TV. He looks up at you, away from the little screen, and says laughing "You mean because *I* can work it, it must be *easy*!" Bono, Mr. Technically Illiterate, has got the gist of his Apple Powerbook, well able to get the song he wants onto the screen, messing with rhyme and sometimes reason on the lyrics. "Two fingers" he says, "and you know Beep, you can say a lot with two fingers!"

The lead from his machine - use batteries,baby! - is straining from the power socket in the wall, stretched to breaking point. Snap! The lead comes out of the machine. "Oh God," says Bono semi-nonplussed and half-freaked, "I've lost the last fifteen minutes ..."

And it's another afternoon ... the light is

streaming down from the skylight, illuminating The Factory control room where the Mexican flag is now pinned to the wall. Edge, his foot pumping the wah wah pedal, is overdubbing acoustic guitar onto 'Hold Me, Thrill Me, Kiss Me, Kill Me'. "I'm trying to make it sound sexy" laughs Edge. "What should I be thinking about?"

Bono comes back into the room and Edge reports "Unfortunately, I made it sound like U2". "U2?" retorts Bono, laughing, his eyes twinkling at Edge who twinkles back. "U2?" repeats Bono, "what would they know about sleaze?"

Fast forward: Bono's sitting beside you on the sofa, his lyrics on the floor, his right hand holding the microphone close to his lips, singing softly to a melody of quicksand. You recognize it as the Sinatra song. It might be about an *angel* now. After seeing the rough cut of the new Wim Wenders movie 'Faraway, So Close!' this song has changed direction to 'Stay'. "Red light, blue morning, you stumble out of a hole in the ground, a vampire or a victim, depending on who's around ..." and as the voice paints these strange and unsettling pictures his left hand reaches across his chest and pulls at his right lapel, the fingers grasping the jacket till the knuckles are white, the singer transported. There's a silence and then as if awakening from a sleepwalk he brings himself back to his physical surroundings. He blinks, smiles, safe now, says "Who was I for the last few minutes?"

Edge rises to the occasion. "Let's play the psycho country mix!"

You glance to your left and there's Brian Eno standing there, taking it all in, making a visitation. He removes his beret, peers down at his notebook and smiles in a mysterious way.

"Hmm" he says.

We're off to nowhere and Tim doesn't like it. He turns from his seat in the front of the van. "Now you just be careful. And let me look after things".

Bono and Edge and Suzanne and a wrecked Boogaloo nod lamely. It's Boogaloo's fault, anyway. He's been corresponding with Mavis Staples ever since they met in London when she was touring with Prince - Mavis Staples, gospel queen and Pop Staples' daughter in The Staple Singers, the voice that sang 'Respect Yourself' and talked of black pride and marching with Doctor Martin Luther King and singing "It's a long walk to D.C., but I got my marchin' shoes on ...", Mavis and you have been writing to each other. It makes you feel kinda humble, a rare thing. So, natch, you've got her address but you don't have her phone number so a guy from the Ritz Carlton, lovely, kind, sweet gentleman, he goes over to Mavis' place ($50 in a cab!). 'Course when he gets there he's in this lobby with no names on the bells and this woman appears with her laundry and he says "I'm looking for Mavis Staples" and she says "I am Mavis Staples". Hallelujah! Give thanks!

So when Mavis rings you up you hip her to what all the drama is about. Gospel! Mavis, she's going to be out of town tomorrow, gotta leave Chicago for a show with The Staple Singers. But *she* knows. *Gospel? Mavis* knows ...

So Praise The Lord, you're in the van Sunday morning and you arrive at the church having travelled through somewhere that looks like it's been bombed, looted and left to rot. Here isn't exactly uptown, either. It's *brilliant*. Rockin' preacher, a white cat for Godsake!

And afterwards you want to stop somewhere to eat but Tim doesn't like it, doesn't like it at all. "There's food back at the hotel" he says but he knows that isn't the vibe. You insist, and Bono, Edge and Suzanne ... and Tim ... follow you into Pat and Kim's Soul Food Diner.

It's cool. Working folk in their Sunday threads and five honkies from out of town, having their breakfast. "I hope" says Bono "that these folks don't think we're ... eh ... you know, on a field trip."

Naw, man. Just goin' t' church.

Christina's in an intoxification of excitement. She can't believe it, not really. We're off to see Pearl Jam, this really happening group outta Seattle.

So we clamber into the van, Christina and Edge and Adam and Larry and King Boogaloo and we're whizzed to The Metro Club, snuck in through a shop at the side that's owned by the same people and sells sorta hippyish stuff and Tibetan death's head beads like you got in Atlanta. Up some stairs. Christina's almost hyperventilating, hand to her pale throat like she's just about to see the Son of God. (Doesn't she see him singing lead vocals with U2 every day for Chrissakes!)

We're plonked on a space of our own on the side of the balcony. The people beside us, they're cool. The odd screech and lotsa waving and trying to make eye contact but

nothin' too much, nothin' too wild.

Below us, it's like Dante's Inferno on dodgy acid. *Brilliant*. Moshing is the vibe here tonight, moshing and Pearl Jam, folk clambering onto the stage and jumping off and landing on the crowd like 90's Jesuses walking on the water 'cept they're lying on their backs, arms outstretched, being carried by the waves of seething humanity.

'Course sometimes the supposedly-supportive bodies underneath part like the Red Sea and you see a pair of boots attached to waving legs sticking up out of the crowd, their hapless and visually-headless owners making like they've already reached Australia. Iggy Pop probably invented moshing, just like dear Sid Vicious created the pogo - jumping vertically up and down like a trapped lemming. Iggy, he'd virtually *stroll* across his audiences miraculously as The Stooges pumped out their sharp amphetamine million-miles-an-hour snarl of rock'n'roll, the tranced-out Iggites literally raising their palms to create a handy pathway for their bug-eyed hero. There's a tradition of this lunacy - don't you remember our very own super hero clambering up and down curtains and jumping off balconies like our new friend Eddie Vedder is doing here tonight? That was ten years ago. That's a long time.

Pearl Jam are *steamin'* and it's so hot with sweat runnin' down everyone's faces that it's amazing everybody here at The Metro doesn't just *melt*. And down below, the world and its cousin is in full mosh mania, Pearl Jam's singer Eddie Vedder often giving a helping shove to members of the audience returning to the bubbling throng. Pearl Jam, they're playing stuff from their album 'Ten' and when they do their single 'Alive' everyone goes completely bonkers, girls are screaming and reaching out to touch Eddie who's a mixture of shy and aw-shucks reluctant rock star and Mike and Stone the two guitarists are pumping out a cross between melody and grunge, bastard Godson of punk and heavy metal, stingin' like a bee. Lord, Eddie's got a powerful emotive voice kinda like the young Stevie Winwood.

After the set you get to meet the guys, you'n'Edge'n'Christina who's gone to heaven. They're sweet as pie, Pearl Jam, and offer you slices of carrot to eat. The bassplayer Jeff Ament, who does Pearl Jam's artwork, stuff that visually shines in a swamp of ineptitude, he's a particular gas. Mike has on a Muddy Waters T-shirt. Chicago. Yeah, man. Perfect. Here in the windy city Muddy Waters often sang "The blues had a baby and they called it rock'n'roll" and among those great grandchildren are Pearl Jam - abrasive, warm, huggable as a teddybear masquerading as a porcupine.

Someone says Albert King is playing in town.

So you're at Blues Etcetera with Edge and Christina and you blag your way into Mr. King's dressing room and then you want to take a picie of Albert'n'Edge which agitates Albert who's already well twitchy, sitting there in his glasses and puffin' his pipe and now sayin' "No man no pictures". "May I take one of your guitar then, please?" "Oh okay" Albert King says, not exactly over the moon.

And now on the tiny stage this towering blues master, almost seventy years old and six feet and four inches of anger barely contained beneath the surface and in his hands his glittering left-handed Flying V. BB King, he calls his guitar Lucille. Albert calls his Lucy and he's bluespower personified, he and Lucy telling their tale, songs of loneliness and the big hurt and wicked men and even more wicked wicked women. Bad times, but bad times is better than worse.

Edge is grinning and Mike from Pearl Jam has arrived and they're marvelling at their peer on stage and Albert King, he's playing the intro to his song 'Born Under A Bad Sign' and now he's singing, all world-weary but defiant too, ain't nobody goin' t'fuck with this cat, Albert King he's singing "If I didn't have bad luck, I wouldn't have no luck at all".

Beautiful, baby.

Albert King
Born: Indianola, Mississippi, 25th April 1923
Died: Memphis, Tennesse, 21st December 1992

"**I**s there somewhere chill to hang near to here or mebbe a cab ride away? Y'know, like mebbe a river and greenness and quiet, bit of the ol' nature vibe?"

You're looking for somewhere away from the madness."Actually, the perfect place is just a bit of a walk away" one of the fans says in response to your query. You'n'Edge, you're sitting at a little round table outside a cafe in Little Five Points in Atlanta.

"..... So what happened between you and Patsy?" You know it's nice of Edge to ask but you don't know the answer to his question. Still maybe that's why you feel so close to him at the moment. He wants to talk about these things.

Earlier, you'd escaped security and jumped a cab from the Ritz Carlton in Buckhead to Little Five Points, the uh, groovy hang-out area of Atlanta. Went into The Junkman's Daughter on the corner of Euclid Avenue, spotted a wild waistcoat with Elvis's face on the back made out of one of those wonderful tacky velveteen towel thingies that they sell at the side of the road in Texas for

five bucks. Elvis! How much? Forty dollars. Gimme, please.

Across the road to Princess Pamela's. The necklace of little human skulls fashioned from yak bone, from Tibet. How much? Forty dollars. Done. Edge buys Mexican holy knick-knacks - tasteless, vulgar, shiny, garish, **brilliant**, the BVM meets Gary Glitter to play 'La Bamba'. Buys himself a Mexican bottle covered in beads which is so kitsch he has to buy you one, too. Over to the Yacht Club pub - downhome no major twitch out, cool. A few people ask Edge for autographs as we bop to shop but it ain't no big thang. Bump into Adam and Larry who are sitting mostly unnoticed out in the sun. Then, Edge and Beep, coffee and herbal tea respectively. Where to go? Ah yeah, forward to nature.

Away from the hustle-bustle of Little Five Points, down roads with wooden houses with wooden porches with porch swings on them, the only sound the creak of the chains as the swings swing gently, their elderly owners surveying the world with a contented detachment. Down green lanes ... across a major road ... some modern functional non-unattractive low-slung buildings ... we're in The Jimmy Carter Center For International Understanding. Through the grounds we walk around the building to the Japanese Gardens, a gift from the Japanese Government. I think we got one in Dublin too.

A stream ripples over rocks. Camped on the grass amidst this tranquillity, guru Edge talks softly to the four fans who are gathered quietly round him. There's serenity here, stillness, calm. And wet arse from the damp grass.

And as we're walking back, you hear this sound like maybe Charlie Parker or John Coltrane. It's coming from a tree, little runs all sweet and lonely and echoes of sadness, then bursting into a maelstrom of joy, all celebration. "What is that bird?" you ask a passer-by in a crisp business suit who's carrying a crisp business briefcase. "That", he says, "is a nightingale."

'A Nightingale Sang In Berkeley Square'. Now you understand a little bit better. The nightingale: the most beautiful, sad and uplifting music made by any bird on this planet.

serenity

stillness

calm

March 4th 1992, Atlanta

That night you'n'Patsy'n'Edge, with Tim on minding duty, you pop down to Underground Atlanta to Blues Harbor to check out Jimmy Rogers. Jimmy Rogers, he played second guitar in Muddy Waters' band, Jimmy the elderly statesman of the blues and one-time staple of the Chess Chicago scene.

A woman approaches our table, asking Edge to get up and jam. She's persistent but Edge, he isn't going for it. "I'm not really a blues player" says this man who's traded many a lick with BB King. Knowing Edge, you can tell he's not playing hard to get, he's just being hard to get. Edge, he's like that.

Now you'n'Patsy are on the dance floor, shakin' out the achin'. There's a flurry to your left and it's Edge jumping into the fray, arms goin' like pistons, rockin'. Out of the corner of your eyes you can see people watching, nudging their neighbours. Who cares? You'n'Patsy'n'Edge, you're into your dance trance and ain't nothin' going' to stop you now, no way ...

August 21st 1992, Four Seasons Hotel, Boston

Edge: "Embarrassing moment! My room overlooks the park and yesterday during the afternoon I'd opened up all the blinds and taken back the curtains so I could look out over the park. Come nightfall I was grooving to some rap record in my room, bopping around the room for maybe half an hour. I don't know what I was doing, just messing around ... and at one stage I looked out of the window and there were about two hundred people looking up, clapping, applauding my dancing. That was funny."

February 10th 1992, Dublin

You're in STS Studios in Dublin. Larry and Adam and Edge are squashed into the little sofa, Bono is perched on a swivelling stool next to the mixing desk beside the track's co-producer Paul Barrett. The band, they're playing back 'Salomé', all glam rock vibes like straight off Top Of The Pops in 1972. Cool. Bono, he thinks Edge's guitar solo isn't great, tells Edge he doesn't like it. The solo, it's like Chris Spedding playing on an Alvin Stardust record or something, a really cool solo and Edge chirping in on backing vocals, singing "Shake it, shake it, Salomé." Now Bono's worried about the number of times Bono sings the word "baby". Larry leaves. Adam leaves. Bono's still worried about the number of times Bono sings the word "baby". Bono leaves. Now it's just Edge, Edge and Paul. By pushing a button, Paul can miraculously repeat a verse, repeat a chorus, delete a word, delete a couple of words. Edge throws some babies away. This is a cool glam rockabilly song, Edge's strident guitar, jagged but warm, perfect no matter what Bono says. Edge throws some more babies away. Edge leaves.

Edge, he's a perfectionist. "I'd like to remix every U2 album" he says one night. Edge is the good-looking boffin with great cheekbones, eyes gentle and intense at the same time, a mind that can find a bunch of wires and build a spaceship.

April 2nd 1992, Louisiana swamps

As we glide past a somnolescent 'gator floating by like a harmless log - it's those yellow eyes that give it away, those sneaky eyes just above water level - Edge is telling a yarn about the great Iggy.

Back in Ireland years ago ... the postman doesn't always ring twice, so Edge bounces to the door still playing his guitar. He somehow manages to open the door and sign for the package, while all the time strumming at his instrument, determinedly not letting go of the riff that has come to him. He knows that if he stops for a minute he might lose it, might lose the mood and lose this music.

Edge, he's been steamin' on the old Iggy And The Stooges rant '1969', giving the chords a bit of stick. He knows he's onto something. Now, years later, after the

resultant song has been one of U2's biggest hits, here in the muggy swamps of Louisiana Edge laughs and says "Everyone thinks we took it from a Bo Diddley beat, but it came out of Iggy that morning." The song that Edge is talking about is 'Desire'.

August 23rd 1992, Four Seasons Hotel, Boston

One evening in Boston - well, morning actually, about 4 o'clock - Edge goes down to see the fans. They've been waiting outside the hotel, some of them for three or

four days. No sleep, not much to eat, just high on the adrenaline of maybe getting an autograph or a glimpse of Bono or Adam or Larry or Edge. "When it gets to a lot of people it becomes almost impossible, because for a start it's dangerous" notes Edge, "and secondly you'd be there for an hour and unfortunately our schedule does not allow for an hour of

hanging outside the hotel. But sometimes you can make a gesture, a small kind of gesture of thanks ..."

So it's four in the morning and Edge comes out and at first there's pandemonium with the girls screaming and just going crazy. And Edge calms them down and he's got a big silver tray laden with food from the hospitality room. "It was funny" Edge recalls, "some of them actually wrapped up whatever it was, like apple pie or something, they wrapped it up. They weren't going to eat it, they were going to frame it!"

EDGE IS THE SONIC YOUTH OF U2 AND HIS AURA IS AN AIR OF DETACHED MYSTERY. YOU CAN IMAGINE HIM BEING A CALM AND VERY HONEST MEDICINE SELLER IN THE OLD WEST. HE WOULDN'T BE A CON MAN.

August 17th 1992, Four Seasons Hotel, Washington DC

Edge is a sharp cookie. He doesn't miss much. Then again, the odd time he does. Maybe. Bono, Adam and Edge are in Edge's suite with Maurice and Ned who are showing them an early rough cut of U2's 'Interference' video. Ned and Maurice, they've burnt their butts off, workin' red-eyed around the clock on the 'If You Snooze You Lose' timetable to deliver this baby. Paul comes in too. Bono isn't happy with much of the finished programme. "I'm not leaving you much to work with, am I?" Bono stabs at Maurice and Ned. "No" Ned says. "No" says Maurice.

Edge's head is tilted back on the sofa. His eyes are closed. His mouth is slightly open. He's fast asleep. He awakes. "I must have fallen asleep" Edge announces. This news is not exactly a startling revelation to anyone in the room. Edge just grins. "It must have been very interesting ..."

And sometimes Edge will be in your room or at a meeting or at dinner and you'll catch him staring intently at a flower or directing his gaze to somewhere unseen, near and far and bright and invisible, and Edge is completely unconscious of his surroundings or who he's with and ... he's just gone.

We congregate in Adam's suite to view Phil's new cut of the 'One' video. It looks more or less the same although now you get a better chance of noticing that Edge is in the band. The shots of Bono singing in the club in New York still look like someone auditioning for a Gauloises ad while the best stuff, the most gritty stuff, the most sexy stuff, Bono in Larry's black leather coat wandering the damp streets of Meat City at dawn swigging desultorily from a brown paper bag ... that's the stuff that should've been *packed* in, images of uncertainty and an almost eloquent sadness. Instead, there's Phil's teasing flashes of handheld live performance - exciting, cheap looking, rocking - swamped by El Bono puffing at his cigarillo sitting at the table and moodily emoting into the camera.

Throughout the screening Larry, who's sitting next to you on the arm of the sofa, says nothing. He views the video a couple of times in complete silence as everyone else jabbers away, then gets up and makes the most relevant point of the evening. "It's too male-female" Larry observes. "The other day at the gig there were these two gay guys holding a big banner with the word 'One'. It's a pity not to have the gay community represented, it seemed to mean so much to them".

Larry leaves the suite and while Bono, Edge, Paul and Phil throw a confetti of opinions at each other, Adam goes to his desk, sits behind it and rabbits enthusiastically into the phone.

This desk, it was reputedly much favoured by the young President John F. Kennedy when he used this suite. Beside it to the right on the floor, within easy examination, is an old-fashioned light-up globe of the world.

The video stays as it is.

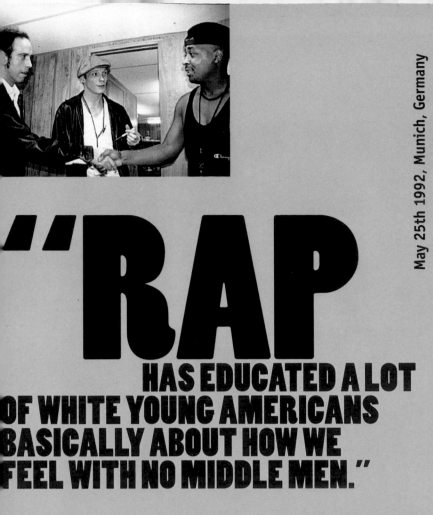

"RAP
HAS EDUCATED A LOT OF WHITE YOUNG AMERICANS BASICALLY ABOUT HOW WE FEEL WITH NO MIDDLE MEN."

Chuck D

It's a gorgeous day. Bono's on the roof of the Rafael Hotel beside the pool in his ubiquitous white towel, eating a late breakfast/late lunch/early tea. "I've been thinking about this idea of having Public Enemy on some of the dates in America" he says as you steal his chips and have eaten almost half of them before you say "I hope you don't mind" and then eat nearly all the rest. "I'm worried" says Bono, referring not to his vanquished and vanished French fries but to the suggested notion of having PE tour with U2. "Well actually I'm not worried but everyone else seems to be: promoters, agents, I guess people who own the stadiums - they don't want a fuss, these stadiums are usually in the funky part of town. We've got some problems ... what if the gangs get into the gigs and we've got trouble. And what if the gangs *don't* get in - what's the point? What do you think O Great One?"

"Well my son, I'm mad for it as you know. Shouldn't just focus on the negative side. Public Enemy are one of the most important American voices, not just black America but *all* America, and they need to be heard whatever the context. If the U2 whitey audience don't dig

it - tough. You've spoken to Chuck D about this?"

"Yeah, I have, he really wants to do it ..."

"Then do it."

"It's a pain in the arse that there's still ... *still* this apartheid in America in music. We've got to try and break it down a bit. Public Enemy are *the* most conscious American rock rap act right now. If we can get together with them we'll make a few points - one, we blur the black and white thing, two, we blur the rock and rap thing, three, we get them onto a stage when in most towns they're banned from playing." Bono points over to another man wearing a towel around his waist. "Hey, Adam, what d'you reckon about having Public Enemy doing some gigs with us?"

Adam lowers himself down on to one of the sunbeds. "I'm up for it" he says.

Bono calls Jerry Mele over, runs the idea past him.

"Oh, no problem, boss" says Jerry quick as a light. "We did the security on the tour by Public Enemy and Anthrax and we handled that just fine. They're a serious operation."

"Yeah" says Bono. "Now all we have to do is convince Edge."

"Chuck D can get in your face but you know he's got something to say and you *know* he means it, man. Listen, we came out of punk music and it was our *job* to get in people's faces. I don't think we did it half as expertly in 1976 and 1977 as Public Enemy are doing now."

Bono

elvis
las Vegas

November 11th 1992, Mirage Hotel, Las Vegas

The hotel has a volcano in front of it that erupts every quarter of an hour, bang every fifteen minutes. And suitably nearby there's a 76 gas station proudly proclaiming the message 'Free Aspirin And Tender Sympathy. Ask Us Anything.'

Back down The Strip aways, a neon sign announces 'Elvis Slept Here'. This sign, it's attached to a motel that flashes 'Vacancy'. Elvis slept here? Cor, he must have been very very tired. "Deffo picie vibe" says Ned. So, natch, you go in, curious. You approach the rectangular hole in the wall that serves as reception and peer over and there's a guy covered by a blanket asleep on the floor of this little office. You cough and another geezer appears carrying a plate of

Brussels sprouts which he is spearing with his fork and jamming into his already-full mouth. He steps over his pal who remains comatose on the floor and faces you over the partition, a green dribble running out of his mouth.

"I'm awfully sorry to disturb you" you say. The mouth facing you opens in mid chew to reveal a soggy green swamp. God, the bloke's going to choke. He's sweating furiously. The mouth finally manages to swallow, the neck bulging like a boa constrictor swallowing a small pig. The geezer stabs another sprout and waves the stricken vegetable in your direction. "I mean," you start again, "I trust you don't think I'm being discourteous but I would just like to know if you would be kind enough to tell me please about Elvis sleeping here. Y'know, that vibe, the sign outside ..."

"Oh" says green lips. "I didn't put that up. The boss put that up. Anyway" he sneers, "it doesn't say *which* Elvis".

April 8th 1992, Austin

It's a hot afternoon in Texas and the sun would fry an egg on your bald head. You wander into the Continental Bar, just down the road apiece from the gun shop and the Salvation Army store. Opposite, a church sign proclaims 'Repent Or Forget It'.

The Continental's a little joint, juke stocked up on early Elvis, a $5 Elvis fake velvet towel like the origins of your waistcoat is pinned hanging from the wall behind the piano, Elvis in blue-black quiffabilly, pink face, bedroom eyes, bee-stung lips.

At the piano there's a man from anther world. There's something extremely proud, dignified, emanating from him as his fingers they pummel barrelhouse blues from another age, the hardened fingers dancing as the voice, all rough and bruised and battered, carries us back a century and more. And there's something scarifying about

him too, like Howlin' Wolf under the full moon. Yeah, scary. And magnificent, truly noble. ***This*** is Grey Ghost.

August 15th 1992, RFK Stadium, Washington DC

In Washington DC Bono's messing with his channel changer on stage and a bit of old 50's black and white footage of Elvis, Scotty and Bill comes up on the screens. Someone at the gig where Elvis, Scotty and Bill are playing throws an egg at Scotty Moore's guitar. The next night, fifteen years since Elvis died, Bono sings 'Can't Help Falling In Love With You' for the first time from the Zoo.

Bono on The Three Kings Of Memphis

"I wrote this song for BB King for his birthday the other day. This song 'The Heavyweight Champion Of The Blues'. He's a bit of a card player is BB so the song's about poker a lot. I'm afraid I've lost the lyrics ... I think the fourth verse goes 'If Memphis played a hand we'd have three Kings - Elvis, BB and even Martin Luther could sing 'Freedom from the mountain, let my people out'... It is extraordinary that these three men were in and around the same town at the same time, The Three Kings Of Memphis ..."

"Elvis brought black and white cultures together and rock'n'roll is very powerful because of this. Elvis Presley loosened up white

"Elvis was a hero to most but he never meant shit to me."

Public Enemy, 'Fight The Power'

Chuck D: "It's not really 'Fuck Elvis all the way'. It's just that Otis Redding, James Brown, Little Richard, they were my heroes."

BP: "Do you like Elvis at all?"

Chuck D: "Oh, great talent. Definitely talented."

Can't help falling in love

June 29th 1992, Dublin

Bono's on the phone and he's saying "If you're not doing anything, come down to STS tonight, I'm going to be recording 'Can't Help Falling In Love'. The rest of the band are completely fucked so I'm going to do it myself. Gavin's coming down. Come if you can - I could do with some Boogaloo."

So you arrive at the studio and there he is, King B on the drums, leather trousers, black t-shirt, thumping the snare drum, bam bam bam, whack! He then tries some guitar and finds the riff he needs and Paul Barrett, who's engineering and who's this cool, vague looking cat with a hippied beard smoking a pipe but so sharp his ears could do open heart surgery and Paul, he puts down some keyboards.

Bono isn't about to hang about. In the last hours he's already tried various different approaches to the song from the straightforwardedly experimental to one like a crap copy of a busker in Grafton Street. Dreadful. "All you need now" you say, "is the sound of coins landing in a hat." Bono laughs and moves on to the newer track.

Then it's time to try some vocals on the bam bam bam whack drums electric guitar keyboards track. Bono tries this, tries that. You like the first bit where it's almost spoken, as if he's sitting beside someone and he's confiding quietly into their ear, then loping into the melody and you suggest that he just let his voice go, let it just fly like a Phoenix Icarus soaring towards the sun but keeping his wings intact. Something like that. Obvious stuff.

And Bono tries it and it works, praise the Lord, and Gavin appears, hair square, psycho shoes, Bono's soul brother, yin and yang. Gavin too, he makes some suggestions.

"Elvis should be in there, talking." Bono says. "Where am I going to find Elvis at this time of night?" And twenty minutes later a CD arrives that your sister Patricia has put into a cab, a CD of an Elvis press conference. This Elvis verbal all "ma'am" and "yessir" is

woven behind the music and Gavin and Bono wander off to hang for a while ("I haven't seen him in ages, not properly") and you go to Lillie's where you run into Fiachna and Jaz, then get back to STS where yourself and Paul mess around with the Elvis rabbit.

Next thing, Bono's singing, bloody hell, and at the end of the song his voice is high and pure and beautiful, resigned sadness floating towards uncertain paradise. Beautiful. Elvis is still in the building.

glass of water. As we return to the Jag, Bono points "I used to go to revival meetings there .... the place would be on fire! Studying the bible, that kinda stuff. I miss it ....."

And then we're on the plane from Dublin to New York and Bono, he's sitting beside Edge, and he calls you over all conspiratorially and says "I've got something for you." And all secretly so no-one sees, not even Edge, he pushes this velvet box into your hands. "It's for your vibes at the 'Can't Help Falling In Love' thing." So you go off

Dawn and the search for breakfast. Into Bono's maroon Jag, you and Gavin and the young Elvis, listening to the other Elvis, the first one, singing 'Blue Moon' as the hillbilly kid caressing the clouds of a dark night with the youthful voice of an angel at the edge, Elvis and George Clinton with Funkadelic urging us to 'Tear The Roof Off The Sucker'. We head down the quays to The Clarence Hotel, a recent U2 acquisition. The doors are shut, locked. Bono can't get into his own hotel.

We find an early-morning caff off Capel Street, where lorries are being unloaded of their fresh vegetables. A fry-up is devoured by Bono and Gavin - feeding time at the zoo -plus strong strong coffee. You have chips and a

to have a gawk at what it is, and it's a gorgeous silver George IV fob watch on a chain, just fine fine and very dandy, and there's a little nail notch where you flick open the back and inscribed there is "To The High Priest Of Happiness BP Fallon, Love And Respect Bono 1992".

So you creep back to Bono and lean over him to thank him, to hug him, and the orange juice in his glass goes splash all over his trousers, Monsieur Rock Star with a sticky yellow stain soaking the cocksure part of his rocksure pants.

And Bono, he just hugs you back, warm and loving and damp.

I've always loved that song and I wanted to give it a different interpretation to Elvis' which I always felt was down on one knee like, "take my hand, take my whole life through ..." I always felt he was at the altar whereas I was interested in the second verse which was "shall I stay, would it be a sin?" which (laughing now) doesn't sound like somebody who's gettin' married.

So I thought "This is interesting – I'll play the Catholic guilt version." But the angels do arrive at the end to rescue the day ... I hope.

Bono

Gavin Friday is my friend for life, my drinking buddy on weekdays and I suppose for me some kind of musical diviner. He's always been ten years ahead of the time and his group The Virgin Prunes were twenty years ahead of *their* time. They were seen as being right on the cutting edge of this kind of performance with a very aggressive multimedia concept, and physically they would mock their own audience. It was very confrontational music. The punk explosion happened in London in 1976; we were sixteen and I suppose our answer to it was U2 and Gavin Friday's answer to it was The Virgin Prunes, though we were very very different. People joked that it was like having God and the Devil hanging round with each other, because their music was so full of fire and brimstone and ours was sort of reaching for the sky. I remember Gavin dressed in a very vivid way and he paid for it around where we grew up. He received his fair share of kickings.

Rock'n'roll is the sound of revenge and for us forming the band was a way of getting back at the blandness. I like extremes, I don't like the middle ground. People who work with us think I'm extreme until they meet Gavin, so he really does me a favour when he comes around because he's very meticulous and very over the top about what he wants out of his music. He's determined not to be put in any one category or bag or box. He's been through his Cabaret Singer From Hell phase, now he's like some kind of post-modern surreal rock'n'roll singer. I don't think Gavin Friday is going to go away and I always watch him closely because what he's doing now I might be doing in ten years time. So watch out world you'll have ... "Bono The Cabaret Singer From Hell coming up ..."

Bono *gets back from his 33rd birthday party well-loose on loosening* juice *– i.e.* pissed *– to find*

a cross about eight feet tall lying on top of his bed. A damn heavy cross, baby. Not the sort of thing you can lift on your own,

certainly. Towards the top of the cross is written 'Hail Bono King Of

The Zoos'. *"I wouldn't have accepted it if it wasn't from Gavin". He has it*

blessed *and flown over to his house in Dublin where he promises to* erect *it in his garden.*

May 11th 1993, Rotterdam, Holland

ne DEVIL hanging round with each other

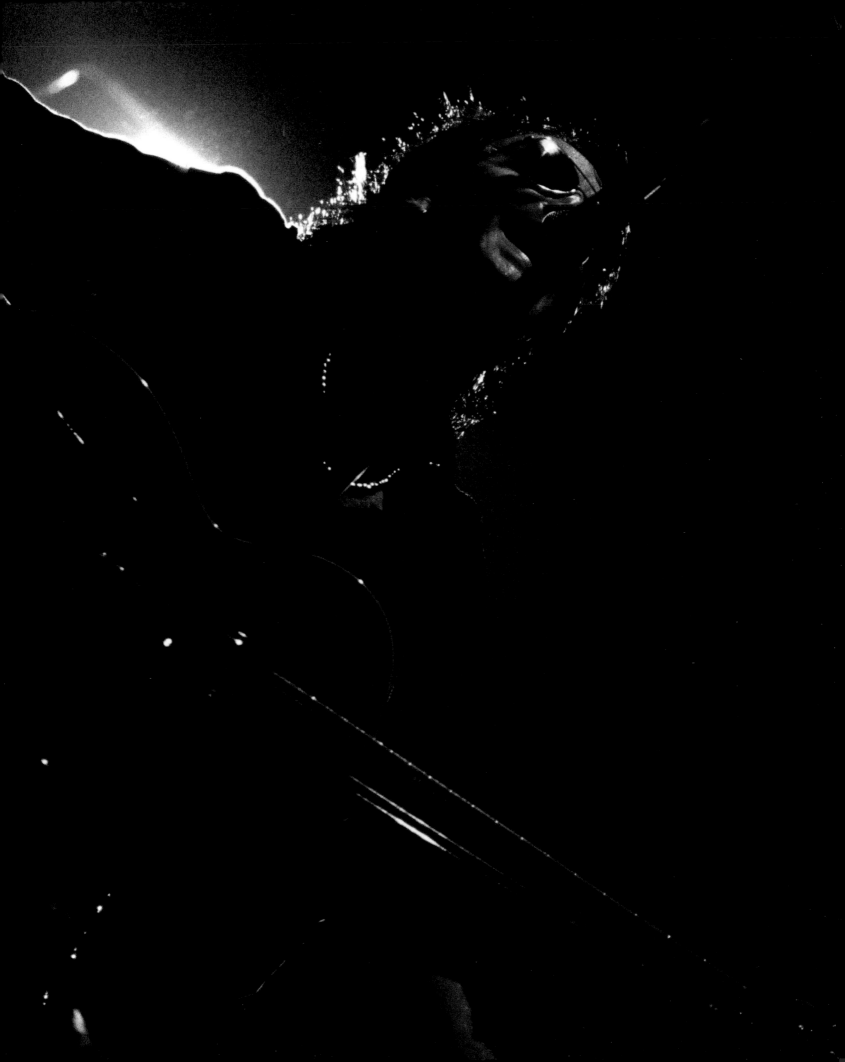

Bono's fucking furious ... or is he? He's sitting here at a low table in the middle of the breakfast area of the Ritz Carlton's 10th floor, for which you need a special privileged key to get out of the elevator on that holy floor. Crystal bowls of fresh fruit, crystal bowls of sliced fruit, silver teapots, silver coffee pots and little silver milk jugs that are nervously standing there on the sideboard virtually rattle against each other with the vibrations of his vitriol. Early-morning businessmen, all suits, black coffee and the financial pages of their newspapers, gaze out their windows in feigned nonchalance while a couple of well-heeled fans who have checked into the hotel sit lurking in a corner pretending that they don't notice the unsettled seething rumbling reverberations emanating from the U2 singer. Bono is throwing a wobbler to the gallery.

"Primal Scream?" Bono is moaning in fake nervous breakdown No. 9. "Primal fucking Scream! They're like the Karaoke Rolling Stones ... on *bad* Ecstasy, for God's sake! This is just so ..." He gasps, seeking a suitable word. "It's so ....." Throwing his eyes up to the heavens like a man auditioning to be Freddie Mercury's

"I'm just jealous *not* because Primal Scream won the Mercury Prize but that they're just *so ... soooo* fucking skinny!"

It's a bad bad day for Bono. Later that afternoon in the hotel lobby as you make to go out with Susie Q to the Roots shop in nearby Birmingham - the Roots shop where you score your treasured Spike Lee Malcolm X jacket - here's Bono sitting on the sofa going completely ape. He is *freaked*. "Fans? They call themselves *fans*? They're not fucking fans!"

"Yo, King B, whasamatter?"
There's a commotion at the front door and the sound of girls screaming and the crackle of walkie talkies and Larry darts in. Moments later, Edge and Tim also appear.

"Where have you just come from?" you ask Edge. "From shooting, shooting at a firing range" responds Edge as calmly as if he's just been lighting candles in a church. "Ah, for fuck's sake, Edge" you go but Edge isn't listening. He's plonked himself into a seat next to Bono. Edge's arm is squeezing Bono and suddenly the singer's head slumps forward and he gazes down at the floor. "I'm sorry" he says. "I'm getting confused. I don't like this sort of new fan. There used to be a time when there were more

It's a bad day

September 10th 1992, Dearborn, Michigan

valet he declares "I mean, those British critics ... they're just so so ..... *English!*"

"Hey, what's the matter, man?"
At the breakfast club Bono is waxing lyrical about these whippersnapper groups, throwing his arms around as he searches for the right description. This piece of theatre belies the fact that Bono *is* actually pissed off at losing the prize, confiding to you later "You gotta love something because it is great - not because it *reminds* you of what is great. And actually ..." Bono's laughing now,

fans crashing on the floors of our rooms than standing outside the hotel! Now you get these super rich groupies staying in bigger suites than the band and I think they've taken my jacket, I left it where we were this morning, the breakfast place, you know?

"I lost a book of lyrics in Texas, I've lost a jacket here. These kind of rich girls, they've got *nothing* to do with *rock'n'roll*. This is *celebrity*. It's getting harder and harder to meet the people who actually *listen* to the records."

for Bono....

BP: "In your head are you tall or small?"

Bono: "The stage is but a platform shoe, Bernard."

Adam on Bono:

"I think it's kinda the scheme of things" Adam will reflect. "Although in the outside world it's inevitable that Bono should have all this attention thrust upon him, four of us there's an equality there which is still respected"

"Nobody joins a rock'n'roll band and decides they want to spend their lives spewing their guts out in front of an audience for a living unless there's something *wrong* with them. It's incredible to me that you make this music that's very *private*, a lot of it, it's your notes to yourself, and you put them out on these public address systems. It is an odd kind of exhibitionism." BP: "Is it like taking off your clothes in public?" Bono: "... And turning around very slowly! I don't know how to do anything else at this stage. So the things that drive you to being in a band, leaving your home and travelling onto the road with a rock'n'roll group, sure there's bits and pieces of unhappiness, that's what Robert Johnson referred to as 'the hellhound at his heels'.

"Rock'n'roll's such a selfish thing. You're always thinking about yourself. You think too much. You end up walking differently." Bono pushes his hair back, sticks his shoulders out.

BP: "Do you put your family ahead of your professional life?"
Bono: "Yes, though I'm not always sure they feel that way. Still, if I didn't have an outlet for my own madness I would probably just take it home with me and end up driving them all out." In even more sanguine moments Bono will admit "Sometimes at home ... I feel a little like a tourist ... they get on so well without me." Bono and Ali's marriage is largely what keeps him sane. He not only loves her but is a fan of hers, admires her enormously. Should Bono ever waft into the clouds, Ali will bring him back down to earth, the soft punch if necessary. Her independence ... you suspect Bono needs Ali more than she needs him.

BP: "Do you get lonely on the road?"
Bono: "Yes but it's the sort of loneliness a *spoilt* brat has that's been put outside the door. We've got this small town on the road and I *love* a lot of these people and I think each and everyone of them would let me in if I knocked on their door. That's not loneliness is it?"

April 23rd 1993, Dublin

Bono takes you aside during the making of 'Zooropa'. There's a telling moment when the pair of you go into the kitchen and are fixing tea. He seems worried about Ali going to Chernobyl to make this documentary. But very proud of her of course, he knows it's up to her what she does, it's always *completely* up to her - she's a very determined woman is Ali - but Bono, he's freaked out about the danger of radiation. "Greenpeace *must* know what they're doing, mustn't they?" And then later, days later, he says "Now I understand much better what it's like for Ali when I'm away on the road ... I can't *even* ring her - the phones in Russia are completely fucked and it's pretty much impossible to reach her ..."

Bono, he's a useless driver. He rings you from his car - his maroon Jag has mikes built in so you don't have to hold the phone - and says "If you hear strange noises in the background, that's other drivers honking at me because I'm going the wrong way ..."

Bono, he's technically illiterate. Backstage in New Jersey, he's trying in vain to get the cap off a bottle of headache pills. "I can't get the top off" he's wailing. "Of course you can't" says Dennis, "it's childproof".

"Bono, do you like you?" "Which version? I'm a nice bunch of guys."

"Is part of you a fuck-up?" "From you, I'll take that as a compliment!"

Bono on Saving the World

Bono: "The first duty of any rock'n'roll band is not to be boring so I don't want to be *boring* about our involvement with Greenpeace or Amnesty International or anything else. There are just so many fronts on which I'd like to do something with my life, but right now it's the music that we do best. If through the music we can illuminate a problem or shine a light on some ugliness, then we do it.

BP: "What does it do to you seeing all this suffering and pain, a different lifestyle to the one that you as the lead vocalist in U2 are used to?"

Bono: "It makes me write songs. What else can I do? It makes me get involved if I can, in some small way."

BP: "Does it make you feel kinda pathetic in a way?"

Bono: "No. Not at all. I'm one of the lucky ones. And it makes me want to use the position I've been given *usefully* if I can, without being a pain in the arse about it ..."

BP: "You were in Africa, weren't you, in the 80's?"

Bono: "Well, without getting into it in too much depth ... I was in Ethiopia after Live Aid. Everyone would have gone to Africa if they could have. Anyone who was *awake*. But I could afford to go ..."

BP: "What did you do down there?"

Bono: "Ali and myself, we went down there to do anything ... The agencies ... there's a lot of Irish down there in Concern, Jack Finnucane's lot, great people ... and World Vision ... and we ended up putting ourselves at their disposal for a month and working in an orphanage with a hundred or so kids. I was given the job of shovelling shit!" (Laughs) "When they found out I was a singer, it was decided that I'd be more use writing songs, songs for the children. So I wrote and sang songs which were translated into Amaric, songs about all sorts of things - hygiene, health, growing food - anything the nurses and doctors wanted from us. We also wrote little short one-act plays, pantomimes really ...

"Ali wrote a labour play about childbirth, we had a big doll with a long umbilical cord ... it was funny, it wasn't po-faced ... The parents, their own children would educate them because the kids would go round singing these songs, funny songs that made people laugh ... because laughter is very important in these camps - it lifts the spirit of *everybody.*

"Ethiopia, it's an amazing place. They say the Garden of Eden was in Ethiopia and when you go there it's one of the most beautiful countries on earth ... on every corner I saw Bob Marley's face."

BP: "How did the folk there react to you?"

Bono: "I was called 'The Girl With The Beard' because I had long hair ... I guess it was the long hair and earring ... I *hope* so!"

"Another time we left LA and were out at Jimmy Iovine's house - there were people there like Madonna and Sean Penn. I wanted to go to Central America, to El Salvador ... I knew some people down there and I had been involved financially in setting up some of the communes. Some of these people had been imprisoned ... I just wanted to see for myself what was going on, but at the same time El Salvador was a very dangerous place and I thought 'I don't want to get Ali into trouble, maybe she wants to go somewhere else.' I said 'Ali, we can go *anywhere* in the world.' But as usual she's up for whatever it takes. She's the one who finally said 'Let's go.'

"It did have a big effect on me. We went into a fire zone outside of Salvador - a fire zone is where they draw a ring around a rebel sympathetic area and tell them to leave their homes. A lot of people don't - and then they bomb them and a lot of people got killed. A lot of very angry people, angry about US involvement backing these fascists. On one occasion we were shot at, a group of young soldiers let off a round over our heads to kind of just warn us, to shake us up a bit ... they laughed. *We* didn't."

"Stay away from him!"

Bono on The Fly and The Mirrorball Man

BP: "There's this chap I've been seeing since February, I've seen quite a lot of him and I've talked to him an' stuff and I really haven't got the shape of him, you know, I don't claim to know him at all. I started asking him about himself and he said 'Ask Bono, I think Bono knows'. He wears kinda crinkly black clothes and shades and he calls himself The Fly."

Bono: "Motherfucker! You stay away from him! You don't want to be hanging out with that dude! He's an oil slick! So fighting Fintan Fitzgerald found these glasses in a second-hand shop, these goggle-like glasses, and he gave them to me as a present ..... and I used to take them into the studio when we were recording 'Achtung Baby'. When everyone would be getting a bit depressed or bored or bleak about what was goin' down, I'd pick up the glasses, put them on and go 'Now I can see *everything*, now I can *really* see it'. Y'know, The Fly couldn't see a *thing* really 'cos the goggles were so dark, but he wasn't looking *round* the room, he was looking *through* the walls and through the ceiling up into the stars."

BP: "Do you like being him?"

Bono: "Yeah, I get to be the poser that I've always wanted to be."

BP: "And how different then is Mr. Mirrorball?"

Bono: "The Mirrorball Man, he's 'the preacher stealing hearts at the travelling show'. He's a cross between a tele-evangelist and a politician/country singer. I haven't quite worked him out yet. But I'm really enjoying his glass cathedral. He's into money and he's selling a religion where you can believe in anything really. It's kinda like the 90's, y'know. It's a religion without God, it's a religion where everybody can have what they want and make a lot of money as well - pyramid selling, anything you find on the obscure channels late at night in the US. He has no shame though he talks a lot *about* shame. He believes in *ratings* - that's really all he believes in and as long as people are buying his TV programmes he will say anything to keep on the air. So he'll say *anything* that *anybody* wants to hear. That's kinda like religion is getting these days. You can have a religion that believes in no body hair, I'm sure you can find a *spectacle* religion, there's probably a Sony Walkman religion - like there definitely *is* a Sony Walkman religion! Imagine trying to sell that to the masses: we're going to sell you a religion where you close off from the rest of the world, buy yourself a pair of skates, put on the headset, you just tune out, don't listen to the world, just look at it. Kinda interesting ..."

BP: "I might buy it ... How much of you, Bono, is in this semi-fraudulent character?"

Bono: "Performers, you have to be a bit wary of performers because they *lie* for a living, they are *insincere* for a living. That's one way of looking at it. They get up on stage no matter what their state of mind is and *climb* into songs, songs that sometimes bully them, songs that sometimes get

on their back and they make it look natural. We've to make it look *normal* that we walk onto a stage in front of 50,000 people with 150 trucks following us around. It's not *normal*, not a normal way of carrying on. It's completely, totally crazy, man. The other way, if you want to take the positive, you can see performing as a step of faith. You might have the flu, you might just have had a row with your best mate, you're gonna go up on stage anyway, you're gonna play a show like it's the *best* show of your life. That's the only way that I can walk on stage. It's a step of faith. Other performers like Axl Rose, if he's not into it he *can't do it*, that's his way round this."

BP: "Are the crowd always with you?"

Bono: "A U2 audience is very affirming - if we don't have it some nights, *they* do, they carry us. Whether *they* do or not I've got to take that step, I've got to walk out there but sometimes yeah it doesn't kick in and I feel that I'm living a lie. It's like an actor. Actors *pretend* they're other people. But it's not advertising, that's a different kinda lie. Coke does not add life. It might be a nice fizzy drink but it does *not* add life. Yeah, performers, actors, don't expect too much of them.

"Sometimes you need a mask ... In fact there is just something a little untrustworthy about people who don't, people who try to come off as true ..... I tried that in the '80s ... *now* when I put on a mask it's in the hope that it reveals more than I ever could without it.

"The only place that's it's important never to lie as a performer is to your makeup artist..."

"MacPhisto came out of this Fly Goes To Vegas and he's still there fifty years later. 'Zooropa' is a kind of chill out record, fluid. We've never played like this before. When you were there it was a rock record. Now it's a more surreal POP record."

You've been telling Bono about the John Lennon song 'Serve Yourself', a wicked stab of Lennon uptightness written by John in sardonic reply to Bob Dylan's 'You've Got To Serve Somebody'. "I didn't have no fuckin' TV dinners when I was a kid!" Lennon rants in thick Liverpudlian on this unreleased track recorded at The Dakota. In Hamburg, you make up a tape of 'Serve Yourself' that on the cassette leads into a conversation you recorded in New York with the magnificent Quentin Crisp. "In America, everyone who isn't shooooooting at you is your *friend!*" Quentin apostulates, all majestic eye shadow and rhetorical oratory. A flower in the hedgerow of the world and younger than yesterday, this treasurable 85 year old English eccentric. Mr Crisp Bono, he's in his white dressing gown again. You know that if you leave the room the tape you've just spent *hours* compiling will go unheard, will be thrown aside as he scrambles into another day. So you make him listen to it, Bono's mouth hanging at John

MacPhisto in the Shadows, Hamburg

Lennon's rage and wrath, our chum Mr Peace'n'Love exploding in bad vibes at his son Sean, telling him to get back into the bedroom, that when *he* was a kid it wasn't so damn bloody easy. "Wow, I'm glad to know that *he* could get that freaked out ... " Bono says as Quentin Crisp begins saying "My name is Quentin Crisp and I *used* to be English ..." and leading on to "*Sex* is the last refuge of the *miserable* ..."

A year later, Bono is telling you how his MacPhisto character is based partly on your Quentin tape, partly on Gavin Friday, partly on Stephen Berkoff, Albert Finney, Tom Waits ... partly on a lot of people ... and he casts his hands in the air, giving a warped benediction like the Queen Mother at Ascot. "You know what I'm talking about, don't you darling?" Bono smooches.

June 10th 1992, Chelsea Hotel, NYC, Bono on phone from Europe

"MacPhisto came out of this Fly Goes To Vegas and he's still there fifty years later. 'Zooropa' is a kind of chill out record, fluid. We've never played like this before. When you were there it was a rock record. Now it's a more surreal *pop* record."

"Being a performer is like having a twitch, sometimes it just comes on."
July 8th 1993, Rome

Bono in his gold suit and gold glitter platform boots is draped across a garish yellow-green sofa in the Hotel Majestic Roma. He's being filmed by Maurice and Ned. Fintan pushes Bono's hair into place, Nassim checks his white-face makeup. Now Bono is reading some lines into the camera, some lines Edge has written for this glitter-gulch character, all dark eyes and bright lies and webbed dreams. "They say" Bono intones into the camera, "He who loves his life loses it. But I say ..." he pauses, Quentin Crisp's voodoo queen gone electronic on mind-altering chemicals and fathered by Gary Glitter. The head goes forward, sunken eyes peering into the bowels of the camera. "I say, hate your life enough and you can keep it forever."

"Mock the Devil and he will flee from thee..."

July 9th 1993, Rome

Bono in MacPhisto drag is sitting beside you in the van as you drive to the Vatican, to St Peter's Square. You're saying that Marc Bolan, bless him, that Marc's vocal influences have their fingerprint on some of Bono's singing on 'Zooropa' and next you're telling Bono how

"Success has many fathers ... failure on the other hand is an orphan, BP".

Unlike Marc Bolan to whom Salvador Dali gave his ornate cane, MacPhisto couldn't get a cane *at all*. So a curtain rod from the Hotel Majestic Roma is made do. He bangs it against the cobbles of St Peter's in Rome, screeching "Shoo, shoo, out of my way, children" in a

"I could have had all of this but I didn't want it"

Marc had gone to Paris where he'd met up with Salvador Dali who paraded the Champs-Elysées with a pair of leopards on a leash. As soon as Marc got back to London he asked you "Where can I get some leopards?" Bono thinks this is hilarious. Now you're talking to Bono about something else, laced with laughter but still serious "You bastard! I'm not on the credits for 'Zooropa'. It was partly my idea that instead of you going all weird having come off the road you should go into the studio and use those energies to record a fast and loose record". Bono replies

voice more camp than a row of tents. Pigeons flap out of the way, nuns look up nervously. The Devil is visiting his old kingdom. "I could have had all of this" he taunts himself in a sinewy whine, "but I didn't want it". He scuttles across the forecourt as the fountains spurt on unmoved and unimpressed, the statues of the twelve apostles glaring down imperiously at this waxen figure from hell. "Ah, Meester MacFeesto!" comes the shrill cry of recognition from some wandering fans. Startled, he signs his name - MacPhisto, naturally - and flees.

January 1992, Dublin Factory rehearsals

"You *always* come at the wrong time. Which is the *right* time" Bono is saying.

We're sitting in Lillie's Bordello having a drink, Bono and you, and he's bluesed. Bono, he's talking about how you come into The Factory where the guys are rehearsing and they're in their little room just the four of them and you bang on the door and stick your head in and yell "Peace'n'love" and there's this tenseness in the room, maybe Edge staring intently into a space a foot away from his eyes and not even blinking as the door flies open and whizzes inches from his face and this loony outside is chirping happiness and hippiness like a robin on Ecstasy waving peace signs and grinning.

So what's the problem? You might not be getting the decorum thing right, however that's supposed to work. The band are having difficulty getting the 'Achtung Baby' stuff right for playing live, a problem that's landed largely in Edge's court. How can he play guitar and play keyboards at the same time? At rehearsals, the computer with Edge's keyboard parts keeps freaking out and freaking out everybody else as well. A technical wizard who is specially flown in explains that, extraordinary though it seems, this particular computer is moody and unreliable. "A perfect new member for U2" says Bono.

February 26th 1992, Florida rehearsals

Bono has this idea to be hoisted up in the air at the end of 'Running To Stand Still'. 'Dead Cowboy' is what he calls the image. To winch him aloft he's a prisoner of these straps bound tight around him like a perverted parachute harness. It looks bloody uncomfortable, and, you reckon, not a little stupid. Skywards he goes, up and down like

an S&M yoyo. So tight are the straps around his wedding tackle it's startling that Bono's voice isn't squashed into falsetto mode. Bono, he thinks it's dumb too. It's dropped. The idea is dropped. Next!

August 2nd 1992, Hershey, leaving production rehearsals

Bono's at the wheel, you're beside him in the front seat, Edge, Adam and Paul are in the back. Bono's driving slowly alongside the barrier behind which fans shriek and wail and wave pictures of their heroes, others with their hands to their faces as tears of a bewildered ecstasy run down their young faces. The screams are an exotic jagged piercing sound, the demented screeching of seagulls at feeding time.

A lone girl suddenly manages to break through the cordon, zig zags out of reach as the security try to grab her. Now she's on the bonnet of the car hysterically howling through the windscreen at Bono "I want to fuck you!"

Bono stops the car slowly, so as not to hurt the excited girl. Next thing she's ripped open the door and is grabbing at Bono who looks at you startled, amazed and laughing. A more elderly Spanish-looking lady tugs at her errant daughter, babbling furiously in Spanish with what can only be interpreted as the threat of all manner of unwelcome punishments. Two more girls elbow the first one aside and hands like tentacles grasp at the "Oh my God I can't believe this" driver. In the back seat Edge, Adam and Paul look on dumbfounded as Bono is being kissed and clawed. Rescue comes in the shape of Darrell who gently prises the inflamed fans away from their object of desire as Bono sits there, half shocked and half luxuriating in the sudden adoration ....

Christina

During the first Zoo TV dress rehearsal at the Civic Center in Lakeland, Florida, to the band's surprise and particularly Bono's, as they launch into 'Mysterious Ways' a belly dancer in full regalia begins undulating towards the lead vocalist. Bono is chanting "She moves in mysterious ways" and this glistening apparition is moving nearer, nearer, shimmering, spinning and twirling, her hips weaving in Eastern promise.

Turns out that the new arrival had appeared at the rehearsals and calmly given her card to Jake, asking "Do you need a belly dancer?" As a prank, Jake had invited her to dance during the dress rehearsal. She danced at the first-ever Zoo TV concert too. Afterwards, Bono took the belly dancer aside and thanked her for lighting up the show. And then a few concerts down the road everybody missed Christina and her gentleness and softness and her contribution to the Zoo TV experience. Packing the costume she'd made herself, Christina Petro ran away with the circus to join the Zoo.

MYSTERIO

Morleigh

Morleigh Steinberg, goddess, who's been involved in Zoo right from the start, she dances for the stadium leg of the American tour and onwards. Morleigh, she's a famed and respected choreographer from the Los Angeles I.S.O. dance troupe and up to now she's been showing a few people how to throw a few shapes - on stage, natch. Now it's Morleigh who dances in mysterious ways, Bono reaching out to touch her as she swirls and twirls, veils flowing and glowing, just out of reach, just out of reach.

Morleigh, she becomes part of the family.

BP: "Bono, what is the bigger influence on you, Marilyn Monroe's lips or Elvis Presley's legs?"

Bono: "That's the sort of thing that keeps me up at night! Marilyn Monroe's bellybutton is a sort of compromise. It's not so much even *Marilyn Monroe's* bellybutton ... it's that I love Middle Eastern women. I think they're very mysterious and I think that in the West people have a really kinda corny attitude to sex and it's

OUS WAYS

very obvious. I like the veiled attitude of Middle Eastern women. Arabic women have been very badly mistreated over the years but despite that they have real grace. And grace is the thing I love the best in anybody. I find them very sexy. It's a very un-American kinda sexuality in that it's not Playboy, it's not tits and ass, it's not so skinny as European sexuality. It's playful, it's mischievous but it has mystery - like rock'n'roll should have."

We gather in Bono's suite. He's scored the two-floor extravaganza with the spiral staircase. The only snag being that whoever in the posse gets the best gaff - like Bono tonight - also gets the parties and the prayer meetings. Tonight's not one of the great parties. Our host greets the earliest arrivals clad in a white towel. We're here to gawk at The Oscars on TV and before the great event - which interests you as much as The Collected Philosophy Of Engelbert Humperdinck's Toenails - you play Neil Young And Crazy Horse doing 'Over And Over' from 'Ragged Glory' which you find in Bono's CD player, then bang it to Neil whining splendidly "Why do I keep on fuckin' up?" "I love that song" the now-dressed Bono shouts from the other side of the room across the clatter of conversation and the tinkle of champagne glasses. "I should have written that song" he laughs loudly.

"Well, dig this then" you shout back. You slap on the CD you brought with you, a new release by this group out of the Bay Area of San Francisco. You've initially been attracted to the recording because it features a dynamite song you'd heard years ago on a 12" by The Beatnigs and only later did you discover that Beatnigs mainmen Michael Franti and Ronno Tse are now the two core cats in this new combo. No one's listening to your new find, no one's paying any attention at all, so you stoke up the bass and poke up the volume hard'n'heavy as this brilliant powerful rappin' cut by the clumsily-named The Disposable Heroes Of Hiphoprisy booms out and the lead voice intones over radio samples and pumpin' beats "Television, the drug of the nation, breeding ignorance and feeding radiation ..."

Paul McGuinness ambles over. "Do you think you could turn that down? We're trying to watch TV."

"I should have written that song"

Adam: "Hiphoprisy we'd been into a long time now 'cos we'd been using 'Television The Drug Of The Nation' which is the track we go on stage to."

BP: "Which was my idea!"

Adam: Which was your idea, BP and uh, when we knew they were available to do the show we were really pleased. They've worked out really good. I think we might try and do something with them again.

Edge: "'Television The Drug Of The Nation' as a lyric set up Zoo TV live so perfectly. We tried it one night, and it was just so great we decided okay, we'll go on to this *every* night. Just the perfect mood and just the perfect idea to set up the show. Hiphoprisy are one of those groups that connect with an audience live. Y'know, they're just one of those great live groups."

Bono: **"Some people call it buzz music, I don't care what you call it. It turns me on, I play it a lot, it's smart, I think Michael's one of the greatest voices goin', sorta relaxed ..... He's more than just a messenger, it's more than just political diatribe."**

And now Michael Franti is on the MGM Grand talking about being brought up by his grandmother who was raised by her grandmother who was a slave until she was twelve...

B.A.D. II

Mick Jones: "As I see it what we've got is the best group from Ireland, U2, the best group from the States, Public Enemy, and the best group from England, in ourselves."

Bono: "B.A.D. II. I *love* what they're doing. They were experimenting with sampling and mixing rock and dance rhythms before anybody. And I love having Mick Jones

around 'cos he's been through a lot you know. He was in The Clash, one of the greatest bands of all time. Only The Clash *walked* like that. We have to be very good to go on after B.A.D. II. That's all. It's great. If you have bands like that it keeps you on your toes, you knowarrahmean?"

Adam: "Obviously we've always been into what Mick's done. He's been in The Clash and he's been in B.A.D. and he's always been a real gentleman every time we've met him around the world and this new band seems to be really kickin' for him."

Edge: "Still one of the coolest guys in rock'n'roll and it's just great having him on the road."

Mo Tucker is sitting in the cramped confines of the Baggot Inn dressing-room, upstairs at the back beside the toilets. She's got a long ciggie dangling from her mouth.

Mo Tucker, mother of five, now living somewhere in Georgia. Mo Tucker, the drummer from the truly legendary, influential, mysterious etc. blah blah blah Velvet Underground. *Mo Tucker!* She's just done a gig here, upfront, singing, with her former Velvets compadre Sterling Morrison on guitar in her band. It's been brilliant and weird, this housewife singing stuff like 'Pale Blue Eyes' and all these young folk singing along word perfectly, worshipping and worshipful.

And you're talking to Mo about her hero Bo, Bo Diddley and the special Bo rhythms and then you hear yourself asking Mo how she got to play drums like she did in the Velvets, that simple no-frills bam bam bam. "Well," says Mo, "I didn't want to play *the drums,* I just wanted to play *the songs* ..."

Cool.

Björk: an angular Icelandic pixie vibe, space child

runnin' through the woods, charm ma'am schoolgirl,

Sugarcube and onwards, forever giggling and big time sensuality.

"Death does not exist but it doesn't want to get down off the clouds."
Björk, Sugarcube

"Frisbetarians believe that when they die their soul goes up on the roof and they can't get it down."
Bono, U2

Jivetv

Surreal

"Abba wrote some of the best pop music there's ever been. And what originated as a sort of ironic, fun thing that evening in Stockholm turned into a bit of a homage. It was very surreal for us to be playing 'Dancing Queen' on the B stage, and suddenly Pete Williams swings around the spotlight and there's Benny and Bjorn standing on the main stage. That was a strange experience."

Edge

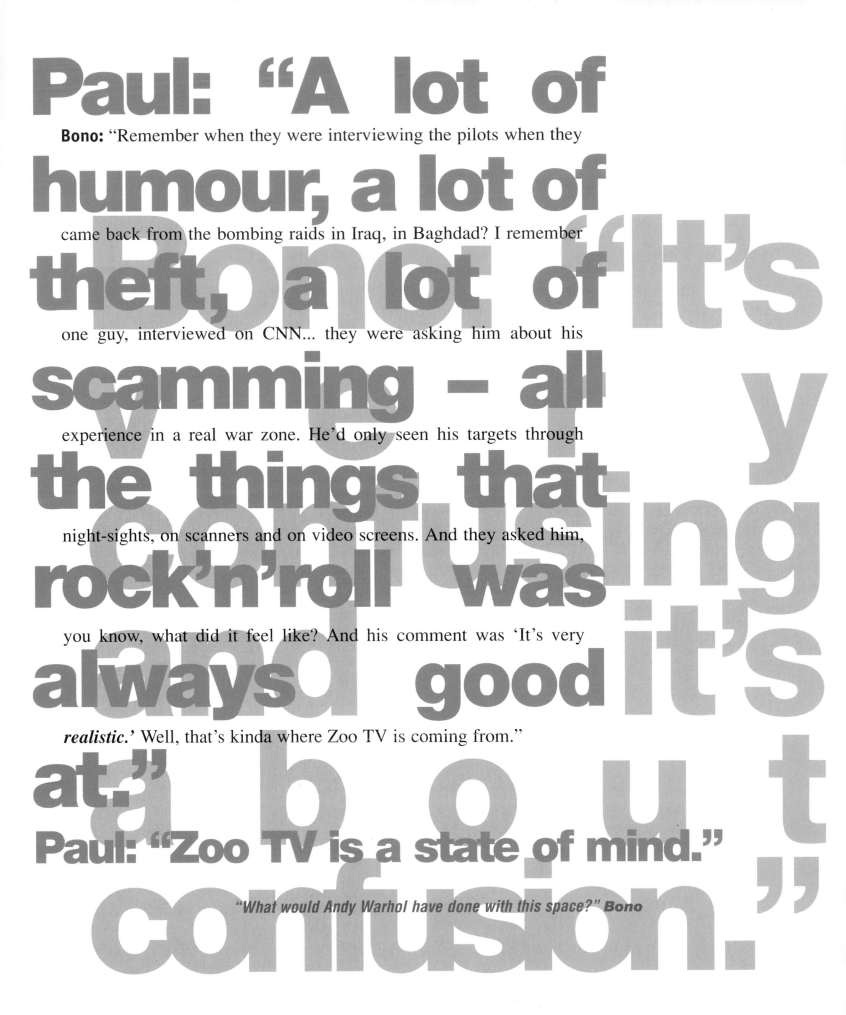

Paul: "A lot of humour, a lot of theft, a lot of scamming – all the things that rock'n'roll was always good at."

Bono: "It's very confusing and it's about confusion."

Bono: "Remember when they were interviewing the pilots when they came back from the bombing raids in Iraq, in Baghdad? I remember one guy, interviewed on CNN... they were asking him about his experience in a real war zone. He'd only seen his targets through night-sights, on scanners and on video screens. And they asked him, you know, what did it feel like? And his comment was 'It's very *realistic.'* Well, that's kinda where Zoo TV is coming from."

Paul: "Zoo TV is a state of mind."

"What would Andy Warhol have done with this space?" Bono

Adam: "We wanted a multi-media experience where the audience weren't just responding in a Pavlovian way to a band getting on stage at one end of a football field."

Edge: **"Advertising and art are getting all mixed up. I think some of the most exciting pieces of TV are the commercials."**

Edge: *"We've set it up so there is almost a conflict. It's almost the Zoo TV production fighting for the attention of the crowd with the band but that's a good tension, that makes us kick a little bit harder to avoid the possibility of being overshadowed."*

February 28th 1992, Civic Center, Lakeland Florida, night before the very first Zoo TV gig

On the way back to Orlando Larry says something like "We're going to have a meeting. Do you mind? Is that alright with you?" Sure, you say, though you haven't got the drift of what he's on about. Then you're in your hotel room pottering about and the phone rings and it's Larry and he's saying are you coming down for the meeting, we're here in the bar. "Oh. Oh, I'll be right down."

Larry and Adam and Edge are sitting round this oblong table.

"We need to get you a dressing room for the gigs" says Larry. "You're the DJ ... You need somewhere to get yourself ready. You can't be expected to just wander around the corridors."

"That's right" chorus Edge and Adam.

"Oh" you say.

Steve McHale, whose day job is working for U2 as monitor technician, is hidden underneath the stage in the labyrinth of equipment. Steve, he's now doing his other gig: MC for the next thrilling act! He has his microphone to his lips as he announces to the expectant arena or stadium, announcing in full James Brown Live At The Apollo mode:

"And now! Ladeez an' gen'lemen! The tenth hardest-working man in show business! The most beautiful, the most gorgeous, the most sexy! All the way from Dublin Ireland! (loud cheers). Mr Ramalama! The High Priest Of Happiness! King Boogaloo and a darn nice guy ....!

"Ladeez an' gen'lemen! Beeeee Peeee Fallon!!!"

"Beep Beep, Beep Beep, Beep Beep, Beep Beep yeah!" from the Beatles' 'Drive My Car' with screams all over the mix, shrieking, girls going crazy. On tape, natch, done back in Dublin at STS. Now Bonzo's pounding the hammerhead beat from 'Keep A-Knockin' by Little Richard that pummels us into 'Rock'n'Roll', Jimmy Page's guitar slashing demonically, Jonesy's bass pumpin', Robert Plant wailing like a dervish, wailing "been a long time since ah rock'n'rolled ..."

Now King Boogaloo is out there on stage in his dark blue velvet gold-trimmed red silk-lined $600 cloak, the cloak that Patsy designed and made while working with the Atlanta Ballet, the cloak with the painting of Elvis

on the back, dear wonderful magic fucked up Elvis, this picture on your back of Elvis wearing a crown of thorns ... your red 50's boots with the white butterflies from Cadillac Jack's in Austin that Hank Williams would die for - and probably did.

Shit, this is wild, every night this is wild, crazy, mad. Audience don't know what the fuck is happening. Neither do you. Don't care, either .....

"Excuse me while I kiss the sky!" Rock down the ramp to the B stage, giving fives to hands that wave at you like octopuses, King Boogaloo clambering up the back of his open-topped silver mirrored East German Trabant that's been lowered from the sky into the middle of the audience ... standing on the Trabbie, eyes closed and hands clasped together, a quick silent dedication to the infinite spirit ... climbing into this car, this disco with four CD players, tape facilities, blah blah ... hanging the Elvis cloak over the back, welcoming the audience to a night of sex, magic and mystery .....

70,000 people ... or 20,000 people ... whatever the venue holds and more ... and when it kicks in you're in the eye of the hurricane, at the very core of love and emotion and upfullness and you look out at the faces facing you, eyes shining, shoulders moving, peace signs maybe ... it just hits you, whooosh! Zoo Radio!

"Television the drug of the nation, breeding ignorance and feeding radiation ..." It's like nothing on earth, like maybe being Jimi Hendrix's guitar amp, these energies connecting, channelling through and multiplying. Ooh, mah soul!

King Boogaloo comes off stage with much bowing and peace signs and blah blah blah ... and standing there at the side behind the curtaining tarpaulin that hides them from the howling masses, this audience sticky with anticipation, behind the curtaining are the band. They're ready to go on, keyed up and hot to trot. Larry twitches and stares at the TV monitor. Adam lights his ciggie and draws on it with intense deliberation. Nassim flicks her lighter towards Bono's cheroot, The Fly's head moving forward to catch the flame. And Edge ... Edge, he dances back and forth, all angular movements and his mind on Mars. Sometimes he lands briefly and gives you a strong hug if you've done a good gig and then he's off again, legs and arms twitching and jerking, his brain somewhere faraway and very close too, spaced out and focused.

the **Boogaloo** is back in town

One love, one ho...

...ly baby ....."

...you want a revol...

And now U2 have taken the stage, they're grinding through 'Zoo Station' and everyone is going completely ape. Meanwhile King Boogaloo staggers back to his dressing room, his disco rabbit and foreplay forgotten. Sometimes you pass out on the floor, waking up in a cold sweat ...

In Las Vegas at the outdoor Silver Bowl concert you're carrying a four foot long cardboard fish covered in dollar notes that Saundra has borrowed from her friend Mark Slaughter especially for the occasion, carrying this dollared monstrosity when Flavor Flav follows you into your dressing room to figure out this fishy business, all the time spieling into his ever-present portable phone. At the gig King Boogaloo plays 'Ooh Las Vegas' by Gram Parsons and 'Viva Las Vegas' by Elvis. 'Viva Las Vegas' sounds awful but what the hell, it's El. Oh, and 'Money' by The Beatles.

As you're making to do a runner to leave for the airport to fly to LA, Ellen climbs out of the van. God, it's fucking freezing in the Nevada night air but she insists on standing there, listening to the band. "I just love this part" she says, shivering in the cold as Bono's voice of mercury in the distance sings "... but I can't help, falling in love with you". It's touching to see this seasoned music business woman still moved by the music, still in love with the very reason we're all here. Fair play, Ellen.

"Ah believe in the stars over mah head and the shiny platform boots at mah feet!" Edge slashing his guitar, Adam and Larry just thumpin', thumpin', The Mirrorball Man in full rant, waving his left hand into the air like a viper with a dove in its jaws, the other hand holding the microphone stand like he's fit to throttle it, the right foot stamping the ground, the mad messiah yelling "Ah believe in the sky over mah head! Ah believe in the shiny platform boots at mah feet! **I believe in poetry! Electricity! I believe in James Brown's hairdo! I believe in the hole in the doughnut, the hum of the fax machine! I believe in you! *I believe for you!* I HAVE A VISION!"** The voice is roaring now, knocking snow off the top of Mount Everest and shakin' the Empire State Building. The audience, 70,000 demented souls, they're roaring too, transfixed on the spike of mass-mind mania. **"I HAVE A VISION."** The Mirrorball Man is screaming, his eyes wide, his arms outstretched as if daring the nails. The music is flailing, phasing, a psychedelic backdrop to lunacy. **"I HAVE A VISION!"** the voice screams for the third time, the man fit to burst with revelation and glory. "TELEVISION! **TELEVISION! *TELEVISION!*"**

Jive TV

Edge: "Having a chance to do anything with Lou Reed is always a pleasure for us, so we did a cut of 'Satellite Of Love' for a B side which worked out so well we decided to put it into the show. And then some lunatic had the idea that we might actually make it a duet with Lou Reed, and in true Zoo TV fashion we would duet not with the real Lou Reed but with a video image of Lou. We approached Lou about it and asked him whether he would be up for it and he arrived off the plane from Japan into New York. Within a couple of hours Lou was backstage in front of a camera singing 'Satellite Of Love' and within a week we had put it into the show. It's a jive moment - we've coined this phrase 'Jive TV' to describe a live moment that in fact isn't live - and a lot of people at the shows think that Lou is backstage or in some TV studio in some other part of the country ..."

June 26th 1993, Velvet Underground - live in Paris Hippodrome de Vincennes - as part of Zooropa '93 in front of 80,000 people

The Velvets: a churning 'Sweet Jane', 'Venus In Furs' like dark, poisonous, warming, soothing gloves of heroin floating around your blood, with Cale on virtual reality discordant but-in-tune shadowy violin, Mo whacking the standup bass drum.

'All Tomorrow's Parties': Cale's sonorous voice ghosting the memory of Nico.

'I'm Stickin' With You': Mo at mike, right finger in ear, "I'm sticking with you 'cos I'm made of glue ...", Mo returning to her drum kit, whacking it some more.

'Heroin': Mo tapping out beginning, Morrison's guitar stirring the mixture, Lou's guitar and Cale's viola weaving like snakes ... "because it makes me feel like a man ... well I guess I just don't know .... h e r o i n will be the death of me ..." boiling life-diluting lava, dark illicit miracles ... crowd clapping like the Velvet Underground are tra-la-la-ing about icepops. It's scary, magnetic.

My my my said the spider to the fly .....

"I have a visio

...Television!"

April 7th 1992, Austin

Axl Rose becomes a fluctuating fixture at the Zoo TV shows. He first visits in Austin, going backstage after the show to pay his respects. A performer of enormous charisma, his face is delicate, *pretty*, actually. He speaks softly and there is no baggage visible at the mo' - y'know, humble vibe. Already, he's been quoted in the press as saying how much he loves U2's song 'One' and you'll see him on the VIP viewing platform watching the group and when they play 'One' tears well up in his eyes as he looks down at the ground, freed by his emotions. In Austin, he makes a point of thanking Paul McGuinness for mentioning Guns N' Roses, for saying that they were the only exciting new group in American rock'n'roll, in his speech at the New Music Seminar a few years ago. Paul is moved that Axl not only remembers but is thoughtful enough to thank him.

May 23rd 1992, Vienna

In Vienna, the Zoo go t'see Guns N'Roses play on Danube Island. The following night when U2 play there to 100,000 people Axl gets up to join the band for 'Knockin' On Heaven's Door'. From Austin to Austria and onwards.

Edge: "It was good to meet Axl and discover that, as I suspected, the real person is nothing like the media image. He's aware of what's going on, when rock'n'roll is so safe and has pretty much gone to work for Coca Cola, gone to sleep, whatever, and Guns N'Roses, some of what they do is questionable but it's for real, and that's rare now, unfortunately."

March 17th 1992, St. Patrick's Day, Boston Garden

Neil Young's standing out in the audience at the side of the stage, watching the band from Adam's side, watching the audience with sometimes members of the audience watching him. "Shit", they're going, "that looks like Neil Young. Well, kinda, anyway ..."

Neil, he's enveloped in an enormous coat of cowhide that stretches towards the floor. His scraggy face is animated, a big fat grin beaming out of this visage carved from Mount Rushmore. Neil, he's rockin' back and forth, rockin' in the free world baby, taken by the music and the magic vibes and the whole huge mind-fuck of a spectacle. Remember, here's the cat Neil Young who toured his 'Rust Never Sleeps' album with *gigantic* fake guitar amps on stage and the roadies dressed in monks' cowls. Remember too, Neil's the man who as far back as the 70's was experimenting with using TVs live on stage.

You ask Neil Young why he's enjoying Zoo TV so much. "Because you have this group on a huge stage with all their TV screens and technology an' stuff, out of reach. Like they're on a pedestal. An' the next moment they're on the small stage and they make it so *intimate*, so *personal*. From being far away, they bring it so *close*. Totally *cool*, yeah ....."

"If you want to go ridin' in the tall green grass, try to not spook the horse."
Neil Young

April 12th 1992, Los Angeles Sports Arena
Name Dropping ...

Jack Nicholson appears in the production office. "Where can a guy like me piss in a place like this" he asks Jake. You recognise him out of 'Easy Rider', the drunk gettin' stoned and then killed. You know zilch about movies, actually. If it doesn't carry a guitar or mime badly on TV ... forget it. Now you're talking to this geezer at the aftershow lig. As you wander off, this hassled woman you've never met grabs your elbow and says "Why didn't you introduce me?" "Uh", you're going, all intelligent. "You know", the woman is saying, "to Robert De Niro". "Oh, was that him? Look, there's Billy Idol". This woman, she's so obnoxious, you're tempted to introduce her to him ...

Instead, you elect to drag Julia Roberts by the hand across the room to introduce her to your guest from Toronto, Susie Q.

Ringo's here. Ringo and his rake of kids. He's just played a concert at the Royal Albert Hall in London when he joined his former Fab George Harrison in a benefit for The Pingas. "I asked George what The Pingas do" Ringo Liverpudlians laconically, "but he wasn't quite sure, exactly. I think what The Pingas do ... they just jump up and down, basically."

Access All Areas

Paul McGuinness and Dennis Sheehan are ambling towards you down the concrete corridor. The pair of 'em beam shit-eating grins and heck, they're almost *skipping*.

"Oh BP, we were looking for you" says Paul, "we'd like if you could babysit for us tonight". Paul and Dennis seem to find this request hilarious. You, you're not so sure, not entirely overjoyed at the idea of looking after some record company rep from Germany, or his wife or something. You point out that you've a gig to do tonight.

Two gigs, actually. "Well you could do it when you've finished all that" says Paul as he and Dennis bounce up and down on the balls of their feet like two loony policemen. They're really trying to get you on the hook, to commit blindly. Anyway, what's so fucking funny anyway. "Oh well, who is it?" you splutter, your words splattering out like mud thrown out from behind a tractor wheel. "Who is it?" Paul and Dennis find your question a hoot. What the fuck's going on?

"Phil Spector" says Paul.

"Phil Spector?"

"Phil Spector" repeats Paul.

"Oh yay, I'm cool you cats, hitch me to the dude". BP hears King Boogaloo doing his hippy dippy yo baby cosmic rabbit, all finger-clickin' verbal bulsh. This is hip, pretty baby, as John Lee Hooker would say.

Phil Spector. Uncle Phil, at twenty-one The First Tycoon Of Teen as Tom Wolfe called him, Svengali producer, writer, *creator*, of teen symphonies and melodramatic epics like 'Be My Baby' and 'Then He Kissed Me', his dramatic wall of sound carrying the seducing wet-lipped voices of The Ronettes, The Crystals, Bob E Sox And The Blue Jeans. And later, the panoramic drama of 'You've Lost That Lovin' Feeling' by The Righteous Brothers and the Wagnerian splendour of Tina Turner wailing through 'River Deep, Mountain High'. And then later still, adding saccharin and sugar to the mound of rejected tapes that became The Beatles 'Let It Be' album plus working on solo projects by John and George, The Ramones to Leonard Cohen. Phil Spector!

"Phil Spector" says Paul.

"Phil Spector?"

"Phil Spector" repeats Pau

You knew he was going *loose* way back when when he released a record by The Crystals called 'He Hit Me And It Felt Like A Kiss'. Phil Spector: marvellous megalomaniac madman and complete *hero*. *Always*. Whatever happens ... Earlier in the day Bono on his way to Yankee Stadium had called you at the hotel from his limo to ask if Phil Spector had written 'Unchained Melody'. "No, it's an old old song - even Jimmy Young did it in England, yonks ago. But Phil *did* produce it, The Righteous Brothers version". Bono says he'll sing it tonight anyway. Now you know why.

That night in Yankee Stadium King Boogaloo opens his set with John Lennon's welcoming song 'New York City' ("Qué pasa, New York, qué pasa New York, hey hey!"), plays John Lennon's 'Gimme Some Truth', John's 'Power To The People' and his usual 'Be My Baby' by The Ronettes. All produced or co-produced by Uncle Phil Spector.

Lisa Robinson introduces you to Phil Spector on the VIP viewing platform that's in front of the mixing desk. Phil, he thanks you profusely for announcing after three of the records that he was the producer "but you didn't say I produced 'Gimme Some Truth'." Oh Phil, mea culpa! You'd see him twenty years ago in the Apple basement in Savile Row, down there in the studio working on George Harrison's album. Phil was always on the phone or on *something*. You say the last time you saw him was at John and Yoko's 'One To One' concert at Madison Square Gardens in 1972, up on stage with John and Yoko and Elephant's Memory, Stevie Wonder, Roberta Flack, Allen Ginsberg - and King Boogaloo, natch - giving peace a chance, Uncle Phil movin'n'a-groovin' and bangin' a tin tambourine too. Hey, Mr Tambourine Man!

Now at the U2 concert, he draws you to one side of the viewing platform, puts his arm around you and pulls you into him. "I want" he says very sincerely as if sharing with you the innermost thoughts of his secret soul, "to thank you very very much for all the help you've given me over the last many years. I want you to know that I appreciate it very much." He's shaking your hand now, one of those handshakes that don't let go, that hold on to show their intensity of emotion. And you, you're wondering what the Dickens have you ever done for this man except played his records on the radio or written about him or loved his maverick genius. I mean, hardly Oscar time. Maybe he thinks you're John Lennon or Ronnie Spector.

Then Uncle Phil is gone, disappeared. You worriedly turn to Lisa and she says don't worry, he'll be back.

Phil Spector re-appears, surrounded by a towering crew of New York cops. They surround him as he stands there on the guest platform, the emperor encircled by his imperial guard. "What's with the Old Bill vibe?" you say to Lisa. "It makes him feel secure" she says.

You're grooving there as U2 blind the audience with 'Desire', Bono the Mirrorball Man sprouting gibberish and rhetoric. There's a sharp jab in the small of your back. "What the?" You turn round. Phil Spector is beckoning you, his finger curling you past the likes of Peter Gabriel, Tony Visconti and May Pang and Lenny Kravitz, the usual kind of menagerie. The phalanx of cops opens to allow you entrance, to be near Phil, like the Red Sea opening to Moses before closing ranks again so that yourself and Phil are like a couple of nuts in an armoured shell, you the cosmic space cadet wired to the full moon and Phil his brain a shattered rosary of fused neon. Two loonies. And one of them, Phil Spector, a *brilliant* man. Phil's got his hand over his mouth like he's whispering conspiratorially but everyone's now trying to hear what's going on, trying to see over the brick shoulders and between the lofty heads of the New York policemen. "You know ....." says Phil and he says the name of someone but you don't catch it. "*You* know Lee Brown" Uncle Phil bounces at a 6½ foot policeman who skyscrapers over you. The skyscraper turns to you. "Lee Brown is the Commissioner of Police for New York City" he says as if you're a complete dimwit. "Well," says Phil Spector, coming to the point. "Never mind Lee Brown. I'm making *you* the *new* Commissioner of Police!"

Phil Spector looks at you with a lopsided howzat! grin on his face. You don't know whether to run or to arrest him ......

Then Uncle Phil is gone, disappeared. You worriedly turn to Lisa and she says don't worry, he'll be back. Phil Spector re-appears, surrounded by a towering crew of New York cops. They surround him as he stands there on the guest platform, the emperor encircled by his imperial guard. "What's with the Old Bill vibe?" you say to Lisa. "It makes him feel secure" she says.

You're walking across the tarmac at Mia

you and says "Y'know, Beep, I really don't

mean?" "Well it's not something I'm co

with." Quizzical looks from King Boogal

Larry continues "It's something I'v

liked.""What about photo sessions?""Tha

part of the job unfortunately. I know the r

band have no problem with you snapping

I just don't like it, to be honest with you

then you say "Alright Larry, you can

photographer. Take a picie of me now." Y

over there by that plane" and he dutifully

the rest of the way to the MGM Grand in s

i International Airport when Larry turns to

ke having my picture taken ...""How d'you

ortable

, then

never

work,

 of the

PHOTOGRAPH BY LARRY MULLEN JNR.

vay but

Pause,

be **my**

hand Larry the Canon and he says "Stand

bots one off. Ah well. The pair of you walk

nce.

March 3rd 1992, Miami, Florida

  **"Excess"**  **"Excess"**

Musings on Mr Mullen Jnr

You don't have Larry's phone number. You've never been to his house. You've travelled the world with him in planes, limos, coaches, vans ... stayed at the same hotels ... and still you hardly know him.

Larry Mullen Jnr is difficult to know.

Larry first played as a youngster in the Artane Boys Band, the nationally celebrated marching band who appear in front of huge enthuasiastic audiences at events such as the All Ireland Hurling and Gaelic football finals and the St Patrick's Day parade. Thus his zeal for making a career as a drummer was born.

His first outing as a drummer for money was in The Drifting Cowboys who appeared in the midlands of Ireland playing country and western music. Also in this long-forgotten band were The Edge and Edge's brother Dik. As Edge tells it, young Larry fell asleep during a gig one New Year's Eve "and nobody noticed."

The biggest-selling single in Ireland ever - ahead of any U2 single, even - is the Irish Football Anthem recorded for the 1990 World Cup Finals - 'Put 'Em Under Pressure' - and produced by Larry Mullen Jnr.

Larry's extra curriculum non-musical role in U2 is to oversee the band's vast merchandising operation - the selling of t-shirts, caps, tour programmes, etc. Designed by Steve Averill and his team at Works Associates, U2's merchandising is one of the most successful in the world, 800,000 t-shirts alone being snapped up by eager fans in America, Europe and America again on the Zoo TV tour. U2's company Ultra Violet launched their line of Bono Fly shades and estimated that they would have sold some 450,000 pairs by the summer of 1994.

It is Bono who will say of U2 "If it wasn't for Larry none of us would be here". It was Larry who put up the now-famous message on the notice board at Mount Temple School looking to form a group. Larry was 14.

June 12th 1992, The Grand Hotel, Stockholm

Larry, who's into country music, you lending him Gram Parsons with The Byrds and The Burritos and Gram Parsons flying high solo.

And Larry, later, saying "You should check out TLC", hippin' you to the sassy young rappers. "What's that stand for?" you say. "'Tender Loving Care'" says Larry with a twinkle, "you mean you've forgotten?"

Backstage after the show there are the usual suspects: Gavin, Naomi, Christy Turlington plus the drummer John Reynolds who's also Sinéad's husband, Wendy James ... Mick Jones and B.A.D. II who played earlier. Two of the backing singers from Johnny Thunders' 'So Alone' album cavort about like a pair of Shangri Las. Yup folks, it's Chrissie Hynde and the equally-wondrous Patti Palladin: girls talk, all sass in pocket, I got my fingers. Fab.

Boy George appears and makes to introduce himself to Larry. George, some years ago he'd said in an interview with Joe Jackson for Hot Press "If you see Bono, and he still says he hasn't found what he's looking for, tell him to look behind the drum kit." Boy George, all grins, he'd often said how much he fancied Larry, that he had a crush on him. And now Boy George is going up to Larry and Larry is self-consciously slipping away, mumbling into the ozone, the pin-up disappearing from the twinkly-eyed fan.

"You must meet Jaye" Gavin exclaims, steering you towards the gorgeous star of 'The Crying Game'. Jaye Davidson sits there in a double-breasted jacket, nice enough to eat. He exudes a calm youthfulness, a calm aura of self-containment, a world unto himself. *Beautiful*. Gavin's talking to him about their mutual hero Marc Bolan. Gavin spots Boy George in the flock of people being busy being happy. One of Gavin's cools is that he doesn't pretend he's not a fan of people. "He's very cool," splurts Gavin, "Introduce me ..." Jaye imperiously like a young Nero calls across the room "George, come here immediately" and George, he pretends not to hear the girlish command before capitulating and following orders. "Ah," Boy George says to Gavin, "I *love* the red horns and the gold suit you wear at the end of the show ..." Boy George, he *knows* that this isn't MacPhisto, that this isn't Bono but then Boy George is such a *tease*. And anyway ... is this Bono? Is this MacPhisto? Is Gavin Bono? It's all a confusion of personalities, of identities ... "Ah yes, Naomi" Boy George says, acknowledging the form of Ms Campbell curled up on a sofa, "she used to hang around outside my house with all the other Culture Club fans. She had a *huge* crush on Jon Moss but of course she didn't have a chance with *me* around! I remember her well - you don't forget a face like that, do you?" Boy George - he's been through his trials and tribulations, breathed the fire of the dragon ...... and yet he remains a truly spellbindingly beautiful soul singer, underneath his ambitions a gentle soul, wise beyond his years and more secure beyond his fears, calmer than the karma chameleon and becoming as wise as Quintin Crisp. Hare Rama, Hare Krishna, God be with you, by your side George. And He is ...

August 12th 1993, Wembley Stadium, London

"Bono, if you still haven't found what you're looking for, look behind the drum kit."

Still Moving

Bret Alexander, often aided by his unruffable wife Theresa Pesco, is the hotel and travel co-ordinator. Bret, he has the task of organizing all the hotel bookings. As you arrive he's there to greet you and hands you an envelope which contains your new key and the rooming list. Sometimes you get a brilliant room, sometimes a suite. Sometimes you don't. Bret's job, it isn't easy, particularly when you drive him to distraction by changing rooms. Still, Bret remains charming, on the surface unflappable. Whatever you say to him, he says "Sounds good to me."

May 15th 1992, San Sebastian

In San Sebastian, Bono decides to ride to the airport at Bilbao a couple of hours' drive away on the coach, instead of in his limo. "Can I go on the bus?" he asks no one in particular. Even before we've hit the beauty of the Spanish countryside baking under the sun, a few blocks down the road he's stopped the coach for vino and beer and Bono, he's singing Cliff's "We're all going on a summer holiday..." and laughing behind his Fly shades. "Oh dear," he cackles, "Dennis is going to be really annoyed at me for stopping. Oh, I'm in trouble - when we get there he's going to be looking at his watch ..."

Not long later Bono has completely forgotten his apprehensions about being labelled irresponsible by Mr. Sheehan. With a bottle of wine in his hand and more wine inside him, he's half shouting "This is great, isn't it? We travel the world, don't have to shoot people, get to play rock'n'roll ... and we get paid for it! Does anyone know the words to 'Living Doll'?"

March 1st 1992, Alexander Hotel, Miami Beach

You've left your box of CDs at the gig and now a long white Lincoln limo pulls up at the front of the hotel. The chauffeur, he climbs out and opens the passenger door and it appears that nobody is riding in this thirty-five foot long monstrosity. The chauffeur, he leans in and emerges to hand you the itinerant box of CDs. Your pal Dave Fanning, the famed Irish discjockey who's over here in Miami to report on the beginnings of the Zoo TV tour, sees these goings on. "Beep! You mean to tell me that you even have a limo for your sounds?!"

MGM Grand Jetliner

We travel from gig to gig, city to city, country to country, in the 40-seat MGM Grand Boeing 727. It's pretty cool, fabulously vulgar even by rock'n'roll standards, kinda like a  flying brothel crossed with Graceland and Hugh Hefner tackiness. Peacocks are etched into the smoked glass windows, art deco lines are carved into another glass panel

and the corridor, naturally, is pink. We drive onto the tarmac avoiding airport madness, climb up into our winged womb and whizz off into the clouds which hug us like a fluffy cotton wool cocoon ...

You like the clouds, like flying above them, through them, past them, the sun shining bright on clouds like mountains, clouds like the desert, little wisps of clouds. White, fluffy, like you could jump on them and roll about like on soft down feathers. And at night it's another dualism out there: dark, mysterious, another world, another planet ...

May 15th 1992, San Sebastian

Bob Koch is at reception, not entirely the happiest man in the hotel. Sheila Roche's phone bill is over

$2,000 - no more calls than usual, it just seems that every time you pick up the phone here in this wickedly expensive place it's another pension scheme down the drain. And the bill that Bob

has just tackled appears to have been more pumped up than a Zeppelin. "So" Bob snaps, "what part of the hotel do we now *own?*"

Packing: bag tag No. 20

Your on the road necessities are very simple: the carpet that you got in Jerusalem. The Martin Luther King scarf that you'd pin to the hotel wall, the one you got in Berlin after The Wall came down. A bunch of silk scarves to wrap around the lampshades. Incense and oils to burn. A flight-case of CDs, another flight-case with your ghetto blaster and more CDs. Tape recorders. Cameras. The 4" Marilyn statuette, ready to pose and pout wherever you place her. An' some stuff to wear. Your stage gear goes with Wardrobe.

Natch as you go along you pick up knick-knacks, like the marvellous 4 foot by 3 foot painting by Scot Mayoh of Elvis tongue-kissing a pastel-haired pussycat. At one point, you have eleven separate pieces of luggage, cardboard boxes, flight-cases, your battered old seaman's

trunk, plastic bags all taped up.

Tim Ross, the security man who also looks after luggage, Tim must love you. He calls in the mornings. "Luggage is being picked up in an hour. Will you be ready, Beeper?"

"Yo Tim" (trying to sound awake)... "Tim, if you could have my stuff picked up last it would be completely brilliant."

It's easy unpacking; it's hell putting it all back. A couple of times you totally panic and ring down to ask for help. A maid comes up, sweet as pie, and gently folds up stuff and packs it and crams it in while you're crawling around the floor with the CDs you'll need for tonight's gig.

The stuff is then balanced on trolleys, sweating bell-boys staggering down hotel corridors and probably hating you, the ping! of elevator buttons .....

It then all turns up again as if by magic in your next hotel room, only to be ripped asunder yet again and the whole crazy process begins once more: carpet on the floor, MLK on the wall, incense and madness.

So you're driving along with Dennis at the wheel and Suzanne in the back, driving along to the production rehearsals at Hershey – "The Fun Starts Here" the sign says when you get there. But you haven't got there yet, not today anyway – and in the car in front of us Bono is driving with Edge beside him and Larry and Adam more safely tucked in the back.

Bono's style of driving might charitably be called freeform, with not the most regard in the world for indicating or staying in the same lane or, often, not being entirely sure of where he's going or how to get from A to B without going via Z.

Bono's looking all confident and winding all over the place and now Dennis is saying "What's he doing *now*?" as Bono aims his vehicle towards a line of fast food joints, a rake at the other side of the road, Burger King, Kentucky Fried Chicken, Wendy's, McDonald's and whatever it is and whatever hopefully one day it won't be. Having miraculously traversed the highway through a small gap in the oncoming traffic, where agitated motorists demonstrate loudly that horns are to be found not only on rhinos, cows and wild buffalo, Bono's motor selects a

burger joint and our hero navigates the car towards the serving hatch and manages to come to a halt with a shudder. The young guy with the glasses ready to take the next order gapes and gasps open-mouthed at the new arrivals, whose driver is ordering burgers and "What else have you got?"

By now you've leapt from Dennis's wheels, which echo with the sound of Dennis resignedly saying "But there's catering at the venue ..." and have taken up position in front of the Bonoedgeadamandlarry vehicle to document this exhibition of rock star culinary aspirations. "This isn't exactly **green**! I'll be given a few more days in purgatory for this ..." Bono chortles half-apologetically out the window as a tray of burgerfied cows and cartons of brown fizzy liquid that rots children's teeth is passed into the open window. You too surrender, getting King B to score you a large helping of French fries.

The server's expression indicates that he can't **believe** that this rock group royalty is gracing him with this display of munching and masticating meatburger mania. Mesmerized, he looks at the shaded driver as if he's just seen Elvis. In truth, he probably has.

Edge is sitting at the end of your bed looking at Karaoke laser discs on the television screen. Back in Dublin, in the bar of the Clarence, this idea had sprung up between the pair of you to uh, maybe, try a Karaoke vibe with the stadium audience. What *you* would really like is to have U2 record 'Help' all slow and have that as the soundtrack to the tacky Karaoke visuals up on the screens that'd have everyone singing along with you as the Phantom Of The Madness MC, Mrs. Mills on acid ... and everyone'd be singing along and suddenly they'd realize the group were on the stage playing and singing with them, "when I was younger so much younger than today..."

Pandemonium pipe dreams.

So anyway you and Edge are singing along to classic dodginess like 'Bridge Over Troubled Water' when you both happen to let your eyes leave the screen and look out of the 13th storey window. Looking in is the window cleaner, held in the air by a rope and grinning, brandishing his welcome with a thumbs up sign like a dangling Paul McCartney...

"munching masticating meatburger mania"

Wow, there's Annie Leibovitz!

up on the wall beside the fireplace.

Wow! Annie Leibovitz!

You go over to Annie, doubly delighted when you see **two** Canon cameras **just like your one** slung around her neck.

"Uh, Annie ... um, I wonder ... would you be kind enough to show me how this thing works?"

Now if it was Edge not Annie he'd have patiently spent half an hour telling you how the thing worked and you'd be nodding your head and going "Oh, I see" but really you

Wow, there's Annie Leibovitz!

She's one of your favourite rock'n'roll photographers, particularly her close to the vein shots of Keef on the Stones '73 American tour.

One day many bridges ago when you got back to the apartment where you'n'Patsy lived in Monkstown, Patsy had beautifully framed the Annie Leibovitz colour photograph of John Lennon sittin' back on his mattress bed on the floor of the Dakota, John strummin' his red Strat. It was from the photo session John and Annie had done just before John died, bless him, and Patsy had put it

wouldn't have a clue. So Annie, what she says is just completely **perfect**. Whether or not it's true doesn't matter. "I don't know how they work either" is what Annie says and then shows you how to set your camera to automatic.

Thanx, Annie.

1980 and you go to this little town - village? Village vibe, anyway - west of Cork called Macroom, go there for the weekend to the Macroom Festival to see Elvis Costello And The Attractions and Rory Gallagher. You get Dave Fanning who's got wheels to take you to the funfair. There's this girl from Macroom who lives in Dublin who's down in Macroom for the Festival too. And you ask her for a light for your ciggie even though you've got matches.

You live with Patsy in Dublin - Bray, Clontarf, finally Monkstown - for seven years, until 1988. Now she lives in Atlanta, with her son Danny. Your godson. He's four years old and he's rockin'! You, you live wherever you land. You see Patsy and Danny in Atlanta, in New Orleans, in London, at Martha's in Cobham ... Atlanta mostly ... and it's brilliant.

And sometimes sad.

So we're on this boat, chugging across the Zurichsee back to Zurich. It's one of those tourist boat things, rows of seats and windows and a little open-air deck at the back. Which is where we are – at the back, natch, headed back to Zurich. It'll be dark soon.

Earlier in the day all sunlight, we'd left the grand Dolder Grand Hotel with its beautiful grounds and steamed across this huge lake – well, it's a little sea – the whole mob of us merry on daytrip vibes. The DJ, moi, he's playing fave raves from his mighty how-to-get-one-arm-longer-than-the-other ghettoblaster, faves which as far as Larry and Suzanne are concerned consist of Abba, Abba and more Abba. The tranquillity of Switzerland is shredded by the tones of Benny and Bjorn, Agnetha and Anni-Frid... and Larry and Suzanne grinning like glitter kids on their first outing ... unit Abba plus two ... 'Knowing Me, Knowing You', 'The Winner Takes It All' and of course 'Dancing Queen' when just about everyone goes ape except Adam who's concentrating on leaning his head back to get a suntan. We're headed for Restaurant Seehus in Stäfa.

Of course it's a gorgeous place, wooden frame lapping the water, a private jetty to land on, waiters cooing, a huge long table overlooking the lake.

Bono and Paul arrive having ridden here in Paul's Jaguar which Cillian has driven over from Dublin for Paul to scoot around in whenever the fancy takes him. Bono jumps in for a quick swim, then dines in his white fluffy dressing-gown. Drink is taken. And more drink. Edge is saying that men who sleep around are slags. You're

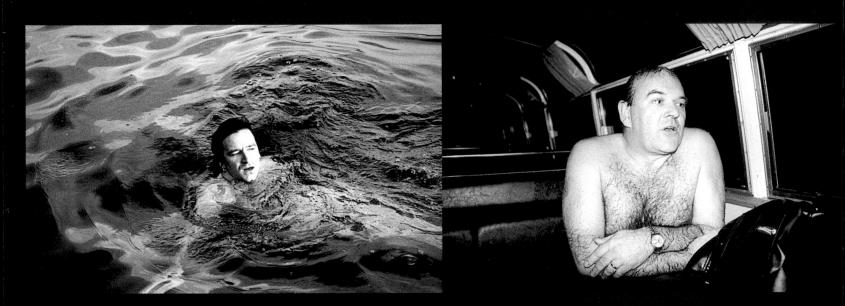

playing the live B.A.D. II CD on the restaurant system. Maybe more drink. You're on water and herbal tea. At the end of the meal, everyone's sitting there stuffed and tipsy and as a special treat the Maitre D. prepares a milky-white concoction in an **enormous** brandy tumbler. As it's passed around, most everyone takes a reverential sip followed by liberal slugs. Whoa! Their faces make like Jack Nicholson in 'Easy Rider', melting into an alcoholic haze. We wobble back to our little boat.

Bono's standing at the back in his white dressing-gown when like a practised stripper he lets it fall from his shoulders and plunges into the dark swirling waters. Paul announces "If he's going in ..." and now he too is splashing around, being swept by the current farther and farther from the boat. Bono's already **miles** away.

The captain susses what's happening and turns the vessel to the left, the wheels spinning in his hands like a crazed clock speeding backwards. The boat tilts at an angle and heads back to Bono. "Come and pick me up! Come over here immediately!" you can hear Paul roaring over the bubbling wash of the propeller as we head towards the lead vocalist. "The captain obviously knows which side his bread is buttered" mutters someone.

Now Bono's on board, dripping, and then so is Paul. The captain's throwing a wobbler, saying he'll have us all arrested.

Bono puts on his innocent face, shrugs and says "I was just looking for the spirit of Shelley".

On the coach back to the Dolder Grand, Bono passes out beside Nassim, who holds him like a baby.

September 26th to October 3rd 1992, The Lunatic House near Kingston Jamaica, on top of Strawberry Hill and higher

Chris Blackwell is in St. Ann not far away from Kingston. A man is enthusiastically - well, chancing his arm actually - attempting to flog this particular tumbledown old shack to Chris, the place where Bob Marley was born or lived as a child or something like that. "You must buy eet" the dread he say to Chris waving his arms in the air. "After all, mon, ees collector's item ..."

CB, Chris Blackwell, he's been inviting you to JA for ages. You've been friends since '69 when you found yourself with the title of Island Press Officer, supposedly responsible for artists such as Traffic, Joe Cocker, Jimmy Cliff, Free. Chris, he's up there as a record man with the likes of Ahmet Ertegun and the Chess brothers ... plus it was CB and Island who launched Bob Marley And The Wailers, Chris producing the records, looking after his friend Bob ... and signing this little Irish group called U2.

Lunatic House here on Strawberry Hill is your home while you spleef and splice together the Zoo Radio tapes. Ah, yes, that's why you're here. Zoo Radio. The aural echo of Zoo TV. Aural sex. Unreleased U2 tracks. All of the band doing rabbit, Bono admirably actoring his way through silly sketches. Chuck D and Flavor Flav doin' a rap in your dressing room. The Disposable Heroes, Mick Jones, Primus ... Zoo shit. Bits of samples including Bush and Clinton (George, natch). A kaleidoscope of sound unravelled by you and the disciple of the Church Of The SubGenius, Bill Kates. Respect, Bill, shining eyes and glowing heart. The programme twitches, buzzes, weirded into snappy cut-ups, William Burroughs meets Timothy Leary meets Marconi and sticks it in your ear, one sound carrot in each. Bono singing 'Two Shots Of Happy, One Shot Of Sad' on the MGM Grand. All stuck together by the beaming engineer Bravo at Leggo Studios in Orange Street in downtown Kingston, Leggo tucked through a door at the left of Prince Buster's record shop. Zoo Radio: rarest U2 CD ever, folks!

Flavor Flav: "Zoo Radio. Me Radio. You Radio." Yup.

First night you hear the sound of a soundsystem pumpin' over the hills, ***throbbin'***, callin' you. It's like ... it is ... the earth grooving. Big fat boooom of the bass, tight an' loose. You drive down and up winding roads with scraggly palms and a warm warm breeze in search of the holy bass. Boooom! We've found the Stonelove sound system, throbbin'. Bill and Childwoman are cuddling in the back. You're drivin'. Bill looks out the car window at Vibe Central. "We are" he says, "the only white people here."

You turn to Bill and Childwoman and say "What do you mean *we?*"

One morning, Chris asks you to breakfast at **his** house - well, they're **all** his houses actually, perched atop a knoll in the Blue Mountains halfway between Irishtown and Newcastle - and there's Rita Marley breaking bread with you. Another morning, you look out and see Ziggy Marley and his brother Steve strolling the grounds. Music.

Jamaica ... like when you went to Africa, to Lagos to meet the rainmaker Majek Fashek ... in Jamaica you feel *so* at home. There's this bitter-sweet mixture of love and pain in the air, the joy of stompin' all over the big hurt, the warm generous smile of joy that transcends the fingerprint of suffering. In that way, it's like Ireland. And there *is* an Irish vibe here.

It's the small hours now and you've been talking on the balcony. You're sitting there with Christopher and his longtime friend Dickie Jobson - who managed The Wailers awhile - and you've a spleef of the finest herb in your hand and down below in the twinkling darkness you can hear the bass boom of reggae.

And Chris is saying that tomorrow he has a meeting in Nassau and then he has to fly on to Miami. You, you're due in Miami tomorrow night too, at the Joe Robbie Stadium to be Son Of Sam II and King Boogaloo. And you say to Chris "You know, don't you just sometimes want to **leave** all this frantic running around. I mean, you've got the **money** ..." And of course you know that CB, he loves this whizzing all over the planet, just a little overnight bag and his portable phone, plastic cards and a passport. It's in the blood, has been forever, since sellin' ska records from out of the boot of his Mini when he was gettin' started ... And now you'd see him watching Zoo and his legs'd be moving, rockin', and he'd lean over and shout "At the beginning, the rhythm section was rather stiff. But now ... !" and the Marley Man know about rhythm ... "but now they're **really** getting a thing going!"

And now it's warm in Jamaica and you're asking Christopher did he ever think of packing it all in, just kickin' back and chillin' out.

"This is a childhood dream come true" he says, "building the castle on the hill." Chris pauses, looks out into the twinkling darkness and adds "But one must never forget where it all comes from - the music."

And down below and all around the weaving jungle symphony is played by the creatures of the Jamaican night. And the Rasta reggae, it throbs through these wild sounds, the very rhythm, the very thing that holds it all together.

Bono on Bob

"Bob Marley is one of the few great, great heroes of mine. He did whatever he wanted with his music, he had his *faith,* his belief in God or Jah as he called it. He had no problem in combining that with his sexuality and the sensuality of some of his love songs. He was tender and open and, politically, a hard ass. He had those three dimensions and it's everything that I want from U2. I think 'Redemption Song' is the one."

Strawberry Hill Forever

Terry was from Santa Lucia. He had soft gentle soulful eyes. Whenever you found yourself in New York over the last few years , you'd rush into his little store in the East Village and whizz up to the counter and lean over to where Terry was languorously assembling a Phillies Blunt and say "Give us, um, a hundred dollars' worth" and he'd slowly raise his eyes to look into yours and he'd whisper "Easy, mon" all slow and relaxed. Terry the Rastaman, he was cool.

Terry and his soul brothers, back home on Santa Lucia as kids they went to a school run by Irish Christian Brothers and they all have names like John and Patrick and Michael, these funky dreads with Paddy names.

In the shop, there is toastin' reggae from Marley on down, clickin' hip hop, wild ragga. There are Jamaican t-shirts and later, expensive uptown multicoloured chunky leather jackets, all rude dude. Everyone in the shop looks cool and chill, skankin' and smokin' and talkin'. No many whiteys.

The vibe is definitely weed. Sometimes you be standing there leaning on the counter having a j or a Blunt when the door slams open and a sack shoots across the floor past your feet and into another door which has suddenly opened and just as rapidly closed again, fat sack now out of sight. Outa sight! And no one would pass any remark about this sack, of course. What sack? I never saw a sack.

Terry was a rude dude. Rudie can't fail.

So you're in Terry's shop on a visitation to NYC, stashing up on some killer ganja, chewin' the cud with the man, just hangin', chillin'. Boogie chillum.

Twenty-four hours later exactly some guys burst into the shop shooting everywhere. Terry is killed instantly. Goldie takes a bullet wound in the shoulder. You hear the news on Joe King Carrasco's Rancho No Tengo in Austin, Texas, and you start flashing on the night you sat Terry down and told him everything would be alright - 'cos he was freaked, very upset

about something - and you'd done your "There's a good reason for everything" rabbit and your Bob Marley "I is I and everything is everything" babble and slowly Terry loosed a little, said he didn't feel so bad now, thank you, thank you very much brother. And then a year later you learn that Terry had been upset that time because he had sent someone on an errand that could easily get that person killed. And it did. Fuck.

Terry was a rude boy. Terry was a herbsman. Terry was shot to death. Terry was a friend of mine. "Ah've got mixed up confusion", Bob Dylan used to sing, "man, it's a-killin' me." You have to dig it.

TERRY · JOHN · PATRICK · MICHAEL

Adam #1: "I don't think it's real at all. I think it's great fun, it's a little bit like when you were a kid and you played at dressing up, it still has that quality to it. Mind you, it _does_ have a reality of its own

before

after

because you move in a world that you're familiar and comfortable with but it's still different to when you go home and water your cabbages." Edge: "The lifestyle that goes with touring? Touring is completely mad, completely unnatural, completely false and when you do it for long periods of time as we currently are, you do tend to get used to it which is worse. It just means that when you go home you feel like you've just gone to Mars because normality seems so weird." Adam #2: "I think it is becoming normal for me and if it's normal for me then that's normal. From someone trying to figure it out from the outside it could well be abnormal but I'm accepting it as normal now."

September 15th 1992, Chicago

Cori Hinton! Wow! You haven't seen her for 20 years, since you were on the road with Zeppo. She'd go with you to the blues clubs in Southside Chicago, the places where people said not to go but you'd go anyway, taking Robert, then bringing Robert, Jimmy and Bonzo, go to places such as The Burning Spear club to see great bluesmen like Bobby Bland. Good times. Cori gives you a colour photograph of you and Robert taken those two decades ago. Will the circle be unbroken? No. Never.

September 24th 1992, Atlanta, Ritz Carlton Buckhead

Robert Plant rings up out of nowhere. Well, Rak Studios in London, actually, where he's recording his new album and he's saying how much he likes U2, that

'Salomé' is his favourite U2 track. "I'm glad that someone with a bit of class is doing the business" Robert is saying about Bono, comparing Bono to Ral Donner singing 'I Wish This Night Would Never End'. Coming from Robert, that's praise indeed. Ral Donner, he was a *superb* vocalist, sort of an Elvis copyist but *marvellous* in his own right. Elvis, he took the song 'The Girl Of My Best Friend' from Ral and Robert, he loves Ral.

Robert asks about Dennis Sheehan, noting "The last thing I remember about him was him trying to march me around the room after I'd had too much Sir Charles!" Percy Plant, now a clean machine, chuckles down the Transatlantic line at the distant memory. "Such a straight guy, Dennis," Robert recalls. "He was never wild, not even then."

And now Robert is talking about Jimmy, Jimmy Page his soul brother in Led Zeppelin, about how he and Jimmy would meet every week religiously for a chinwag, about how wonderful it was that they were becoming buddies again, getting closer after all the madness that had gone down. "And then one week Jimmy said 'I won't be able to meet you next week because I'm going to be working with David Coverdale ...'" Reliving the moment, Robert is bemused - no, more like horrified - at the very idea. David Coverdale! The Deep Purple singer who we all used to laugh about with his sub-Robert Plant stance, a warped cartoon copy of Robert with Zeppo. "Well" you say, trying to soothe the wound, "Jimmy is entitled to work with who he wants". "But it's *absurd,* isn't it?" Robert replies. "Yes, but all we can do is wish Jimmy well" you answer. Not just absurd but crazy. But then ... to be a rock and not to roll ... *Damn*.

October 20th 1992, Los Angeles

Adam's in your drawing room at the Sunset Marquis in West Hollywood and among the chaos and debris he spots the picture of you'n'Robert, you with hair on your head and looking as if you've actually been in daylight once or twice. "I take it" Adam says, cackling wildly, "that that was before drugs!"

There's no answer to that. Not here, anyway.

May 22nd 1992, Milan

Bono's sitting in this underground dungeon of a club, hip hop bouncing off the walls and jack-knifing into your brain like marshmallow mallets. *Everybody* looks beautiful, male and female. It's models a go go, girls from *everywhere* - Sweden, Texas, England, Australia - and Bono's sitting there at this table surrounded by these fall-over-dead beautiful women and a couple of them, they're bending his ears. The one who's shouting loudest, she's saying "We get in free here but the trouble is when rock groups come to town we have to go and sit with them, be nice to them. It's dreadful, isn't it?" Bono pauses for a moment, then grins like a Cheshire Cat. "I rather like it" he says.

August 26th 1992, Montreal

Lights. Action. Dodgems. Bulbs of all different colours. Pandemonium. Screaming. A human wedge pushing itself through the crowd, a cameraman walking backwards filming Bono and Daniel Lanois attempting to talk as they spearhead the posse.

Film-maker Philip King is making a programme on Daniel that is to document this French Canadian's work as an artist in his own right and as a record producer to Bob Dylan, Peter Gabriel and U2. The idea is to capture Daniel and Bono and Larry here in this funfair in Montreal but already the finger of madness is poking from behind the clouds of well-laid plans.

We're waiting to board the roller-coaster, the - as we're about to discover - aptly titled Le Monstre.

On the opposite platform just yards away a cacophony of U2 fans has gathered, threatening to spill over the lip of the platform onto the little railway line. The

sound is like something from 'A Hard Day's Night' or The Beatles at Shea Stadium, a relentless wet-knickered screaming that pierces your ears and enters what's left of your mind, shattering half-formed thoughts in your brain like splinters of glass exploding in porridge. "Aaaaaagh! Eeeeeegh!" You see the mouths open, tears running down pubescent faces, arms trying to wave and not fall over. "I'm scared" says Nassim, and we haven't even gotten onto the roller-coaster ride.

Le Monstre rattles into the funfair station and we climb in, a metal bar immediately snapping up to secure us into the little seats. Bono and Daniel are sitting beside each other in the second pair of seats, the cameraman and lightingman pointed backwards in the first.

We're off. The screeching continues but loses its

ear-bleeding high density volume as Le Monstre snakes us away, upwards, upwards, to the top of the ride.

And then the train stops. We. Are. Stuck.

This is completely and utterly surreal, hanging here at ninety degrees. "We're out of harm's way" Suzanne notes drily as you point out that this wasn't in the itinerary. Now you fully comprehend why Elvis would hire whole amusement parks. We. Are. Fucking. Trapped. Up here on the top of the world looking down at the blinking lights below us, reds, yellows, purples, a pattern of confusion as the steel bar across our stomachs squashes us into our seats, we are prisoners. What's happening? "They just want to see a rock star in captivity" offers Nancy Sullivan from PolyGram who's pinioned beside you.

Five minutes. Ten minutes. Have we been here forever? Far, far away like in a dream or another world or both, we can still hear the keening of the screaming fans. The wind whistles around our heads. A quarter of an hour?

Now you can make out a man climbing the little railway line, climbing up towards you. He reaches his destination, like Hillary on Mount Everest. Words are spoken, up here in the darkness. There's the clatter of someone leaving the train and you can hear Ned shouting out the information "They don't like the idea of the movie camera. It might go whizzing up in the air and chop a few people's heads off and they don't like the idea of that at all."

Ah ...

Clanking sounds. At last, we're off again. Are we? Oh yes, oh God yes, plummeting downwards, downwards, swerving round corners as the wheels screech and grind out sparks, gravity now a stranger as our insides make to escape out of our open mouths. Up, down, whoosh! Thank the Lord you didn't eat before coming out tonight. Slide back into the station. You, you've never been so frightened in your life. *Jeeesus!* The screaming, the screaming, the fans are still screaming. Le Monstre ... Oh God bless us *all* ...

Now we're off in the van to Sharx pool hall - Bono, Edge, Larry, Suzanne, Daniel, Philip King, the whole mad crew. "Larry, remember you're in charge" shoots out Suzanne with Larry responding "That's unacceptable. I'm a rock star. I'm in your hands. Whatever you want to do with me, do it now."

Edge is in the front seat chatting to Bono. Edge, he makes to flick his ciggie out the window but it bounces backwards, hits you on your Keef Richard t-shirt. "You've made a hole, Edge, in Keef's nose" you moan and Larry pipes up "I think he had one there before, Beep ..."

August 28th 1992, Montreal, am

The gig went great with Daniel joining U2 on stage for 'I Still Haven't Found What I'm Looking For' and in the set by King Boogaloo there Beep is, attempting his French and including the Jean Le Loup record that went down such a storm in Paris. Now you're in this $1 billion worth of building and you're meant to be doing a runner but the MGM Grand broke down and the other one they sent, it didn't have the right papers, not Rizla but regulations, documents, the paraphernalia of permissions. Something like that, anyway. There are orchids in your dressing room and Suzanne is asking you "Would you mind staying here tonight?" and you're telling her "Well I need to get to New York, I've some Zoo Radio stuff to prepare". It's 1.45 am and no one knows for sure what's happening. You wander down the concrete corridors. What's happening, Ned? "We're sitting around in a Portacabin in Montreal somewhere in an outdoor stadium with a roof waiting for some planes to pick us up and generally having a miserable time."

In the band's dressing room, Daniel is having fun taking black and white Polaroids of Bono and Edge and some French Canadian models whose legs seem to go on for ever.

It's 2.50 am now and the news comes through that Larry, Adam, Paul and party are still stuck on a runway somewhere. Meanwhile you're whizzing along in a van, waving your little tape recorder at the nearest faces. Morleigh, where are we? "I have no idea." Nassim, where are we? "Fuck knows." Daniel, where are we? "We're in Montreal and we're going to have some fun as the planes have been delayed and something tells me we're not going anywhere tonight, we're staying right here in Montreal."

We find ourselves in Angels club, pop art visuals all over the walls and a couple of pool tables. Bono decides to drink quietly by the side of the action, talking to Morleigh. Edge pockets the black as on cue the radio crackles in Suzanne's hand. She announces we're on our way to the airport and in the van someone says it was on the radio news that U2 were in Sharx pool hall last night. Well two nights ago actually.

At 4.15 we arrive at Dorval Airport set among small huts not unlike an industrial estate. In the drizzle it's like making some pre-dawn escape as we scramble down shadowy little lanes and under barriers onto the tarmac, getting signalled mysteriously by mysterious people appearing out of the darkness. "Why didn't they park the planes nearer to us?" asks Nassim as we're filtered off in different directions towards the expensive mosquitos that litter the runway.

You're on a little jet now with Edge, Daniel, Fintan and Tim, and Edge is asking the pilot before we take off "Is that guy Andrew, Hurricane Andrew, hanging around these parts?" And the pilot is answering calmly "Well this is all part of it, this is the moisture from it, this rain we're getting, it's following us." Oh *great*.

On the plane on Fintan's ghetto blaster we listen to The Young Disciples and Edge's nifty edit of 'Wild Horses', touching down in New York at 6 am. As we bounce over potholes towards Manhattan, in the van on the radio Howard Stern is slagging off Scott Muni's jingoistic imperialistic pro-war recording. "If you insist on pulling America into your war, remember this" Muni monotones in his deep deep voice over the oo oo choir, "when you look across the desert sand and see America's sons and daughters coming straight at you, you can count on one thing for sure Mr Hussein ..." and here it comes, the killer punchline "... we'll kick your ass all the way to Baghdad!" What bollox! As we pull up outside of the Rhiga Royal Hotel, home at last, we're saved by the sound of T. Rex on the radio doin' 'Get It On', Marc's voice teasing Chuckleberried "meanwhile, I'm *still* thinkin'..." "Perfect" says Edge.

Another night in Hamburg.

We head for the Reeperbahn, where flesh is the flash and the passport is cash. We find ourselves in a dingy dump where the fake velour smells like cheap perfume gone musty. Larry and Suzanne rapidly depart for the pool hall situated conveniently next door. Here in our chosen locale, two tables away a couple of drunk Japanese gentlemen are having their dreams fondled under the table while the two working girls stick their tongues into their prey's ears and giggle at each other.

The show here tonight centres on a piece popular the world over, 'Phantom Of The Opera'. Having not seen the original, one is incompetent to compare our Reeperbahn translation to Andrew Lloyd Webber's original piece of work but one suspects what Lord Webber had in mind differs somewhat to tonight's outing. Oh, sure, we get the geezer with his face half-covered with a metallic mask, we have the lady swooning all over the place, the same ghastly hit soundtrack, we even get a staircase. But, basically, there's a lot of fucking going on, Mr. Phantom up there on the stage doing the third leg boogie on Miss Whatsername, this position, that position, both of 'em all the time miming to Andrew Lloyd Webber's score. Miming more enthusiastically than the fucking, actually. How many shows a night? Three? Four? It's a hard job. And sad. And pathetic.

"Is this sick?" queries Edge.

"Yes, but there **must** be something interesting about it," says Bono, "I mean, we're still here. Aren't we ...?"

is this

sick?

June 14th 1992, Hamburg, Germany

You've been summoned. First Dennis tells you "Paul wants to see you tomorrow at 11 o'clock." Then, later, Suzanne says the same. Oh shit.

On the door of Paul's suite there's a scribbled note. "I'm in the shower" it says, "Please come back at 11.30."

Finally, you're sitting down at a little table opposite Paul. His hair's wet and he's cut himself shaving. The view out of the open French windows of the lake and the mountains is magnificent. It's hot in here.

"Well now," says Paul, looking down at his notepad. "I don't want to come over as a headmaster but sometimes I have to set out the rules." He lectures you softly, gently, but firm, very very firm. You're always late for checking out of hotels, he says, you're always late in paying your incidentals, you keep people waiting. "It just won't do" he says.

He looks down at his notepad again. "Now there's another matter I need to mention ... " His tone is measured, calm. "I don't want to be a bore, I don't want to spoil your fun ..." Oh God, what now? "... but you've got to be more careful about the girls who stay in your hotel room." BP: "Why? What's the problem?" Paul: "Age is the problem". BP: "Mine or theirs?"

He stands up and sticks out his hand and you shake it and you're halfway out the door when he calls out "Oh, Beep ..." Oh, Christ! "... you've left your sunglasses ..."

May 13th 1992, Beau-Rivage Palace, Lausanne, Switzerland

"Pau

see

tom

at 1

ul wants to

ou

orrow

1 o'clock."

Paul: "I was always very interested in records. I bought Beatles records and Rolling Stone records and I was a pop fan. I grew up in Bournemouth in the 60's so I was a Mod. Simultaneously though, I was always very interested in names on the sleeves and I knew for instance that Brian Epstein managed The Beatles, that Andrew Oldham managed The Rolling Stones, that Albert Grossman managed Bob Dylan. That seemed natural for me to know and I suppose I must have figured out that this was a job I might enjoy doing. In fact let's be clear about it, I had figured it out. I had planned to be a Rock'n'Roll Manager."

BP: "U2 wasn't your first entrée into the mêlée was it?"

Paul: "I was hoping you weren't going to mention that but it's true. There was a previous group, they were called Spud, they had a brief career in Ireland and Sweden. They were signed to a label called Sonet. They were big mainly in Northern Sweden."

BP: "Well, you got a tickle?"

Paul: "Yeah, it was a tickle. I practised on them, I suppose it is fair to say. I don't think it did them any harm. They were the dummy run."

Edge: "Paul McGuinness was an important step, and we went after him in a very determined way. When he came on board it was very important. We didn't want to be a cult group, we wanted to be a big group and we thought that's where our talents lay, that's what we, as a group of guys together, that's what we had the potential to be. We needed Paul McGuinness to help us do that."

Paul: "I'm the only person on this tour who can bloody well spell!"

Bono: "There are four members of U2. If there is a fifth, non-musical, member it is Paul McGuinness. Either that or Adam's willie! U2 is a gang of four but a corporation of five."

BP: "What's the worst thing about managing U2?"

Paul: "Actually there's nothing particularly bad about managing U2, there are a lot of good things about managing U2. It takes a lot of effort and it takes a lot of concentration but it's not any harder than running any other large business. Nowadays we can afford to hire the best people to do the individual tasks and it's a pleasure to identify those people and bring them in."

BP: "Are you amazed at the stature and hierarchial position of U2?"

Paul: "No, I've never been surprised by their success. Now they do very well what at the beginning they did quite badly, but the thing that they do has never really changed.

The four of them stood there and made an enormous noise. That is what a rock'n'roll band ought to do as far as I'm concerned and they now do it supremely well."

In the flowermarket in the Old Town a little old lady is trying to sell you a tin crucifix. You don't want it. She doesn't understand English. "How much?" you ask a passing Scandinavian. "Whatever you want to give her" comes the response. You give the lady three Krooni - the equivalent of 12 or 13 pence - and you don't take her cross and she looks momentarily startled and then this frail, aged woman hops in the air like a sparrow and kisses you, several big smackers on your cheek.

Further on down the stalls selling red red roses, their sweet bouquet fragrant in the afternoon air, another little old lady all bent up and her face lined with a thousand worries, she slowly sorts strawberries in a wicker basket, sorting out the rotten from the salvageable and puts them one by one in the fruit-stained punnet and then stands there forlornly hoping someone will buy her sole offering.

It's a long way from limos and the MGM Grand

here, not yet.

See, you have to go with the flow, to climb aboard the magic carpet and see where it takes you. 'Course sometimes you have to aim the damn thing, and *push*.

You're meant to be going to Estonia on Sunday,

July 3rd and 4th 1992, Estonia

To Russia

and chandeliers like giant Elizabeth Taylor earrings.

On street corners desolate clumps of Russian soldiers cluster in ragged uniforms, broke and their power gone. They can't be recalled to Moscow: there's nowhere there to put them, no money to pay them.

You're in the town of Tallinn in this former territory of the USSR, Estonia. You're not meant to be

getting a lift on the empty chartered plane going there but when you arrive at Stansted airport from Dublin on Saturday morning, there out of the window of your flight, it's plane to see: Estonian Air, sitting there on the runway.

So you find this bunch of people, all baggage and curiosity, who are gathered to get boarding passes: Hothouse Flowers and The London Chamber Orchestra, just flown in from Geneva. One of the orchestra hasn't shown up so there and then you hitch a ride with them on their plane to Estonia. Simple.

Naturally you don't have a visa so when you land in Tallinn you vague out, say "Oh my name doesn't appear to be on the list" and the immigration officer all sweet as pie says "We'll give you a free visa" and stamps your passport. Thank you God.

Independent for less than a year, the big fat vulgar wad of Estonian money you get at Tallinn airport is clean and crisp. "We have our new money for three weeks" beams the cashier all proudly, handing you a brick of notes. If you have £100 you're rich, very rich.

Most folk here are poor. The average monthly

wage is £30, maybe £60 if you're comfortable.

Everyone's friendly, except the waiters. Food is scarce, even in the restaurants to which most Estonians can't afford to venture. The waiters have a disconcerting habit of wandering away while you're talking to them. They're doubtlessly fed up having to tell foreigners all day long that the food on the menu ... well, most of it isn't available.

Now, the waiter isn't forthcoming with **anything** except a bottle of grey bubbly water. Thankfully you've brought some muesli with you from Dublin but there's no milk to be had so you eat this muesli with the fizzy water that tastes of Alka Seltzer, eat it out of an ashtray as there are no bowls either. "May I have some too?" Fiachna Ó Braonáin from Hothouse Flowers asks you hungrily. The waiter is delighted that you've found something to eat.

At The Independence Festival you're sitting there

aboriginal people, are uplifting with their pummelling cries of independence. Kid Creole And The Coconuts are smooth and polished ... Bob Geldof with his band of Happy Clubbers is scraggly and charismatic, the perfect self-deprecating showman.

"So what's the U2 thing like?" Geldof interrogates you as he stands at the side of the stage in his suit of flowers waiting for the Flowers to go on. Bob, he says he was invited to go to the London gigs "but I backed off, I don't want to see all that Zoo TV crap. I *like* U2 as you know, they've written some

with love

with Fiachna, the pair of you negotiating with a Finn for a smidgeling of Russian Woodbine - heavy lawnmower vibe as it transpires. Serves us right! - when this familiar voice shouts out "Beep! What the *fuck* are you doing here?" It's Geldof, causing you to almost drop the pitiful amount of grass onto the floor.

Heck, it's a gas to see him. He's impressed at how well the festival is being run ("I thought it might be a fuckin' shambles") and when he gives a press conference headphones are handed out and BG's Irish is translated virtually immediately as he talks rapidly, translated by invisible interpreters into Dutch or Russian or German or whatever to the mesmerized media.

On stage, EMF are all dancey and swirling with a punkish attitude, so invigorating, the Australian group Yothu Yindi, mostly

really good songs but Bono in those Fly shades - fuckin' spare me! Look, we've seen that all before Beep - Lou Reed in The Velvet Underground, Brian Jones during 'Satanic Majesties' ..." You shoulda gone, Bob, you shoulda checked it out ... "No! All that technological crap. It's embarrassing. Who needs it? I don't want to see this group I like and be depressed and brought down ..."

And now it's midnight and a young boy, nine, maybe ten years old, he's clambered atop a roll of fencing here at The Independence Festival and he's solitary, alone, alone in between the throng of young ladies on their young men's shoulders, beaming nipple power and a sense of exhilaration and this young boy, he's wide-eyed, never heard anything like this before, the might of the 48-piece London Chamber Orchestra with Hothouse Flowers, and Liam Ó Maonlaí, he's singing "Yes, there are many questions, yes, there is red tape on the ground ... a simple truth can cut through ev'rything ..." and the young boy's face all open and receiving, he hasn't been hurt or disappointed yet or had an adult's reason to cry and you look at this young face and you see ... freedom.

God is having breakfast, His once-a-year favourite: Tequila, peyote, and magic mushrooms sprinkled with a ground P bud and granulated organic mescaline crystals. God, He's *loose* today, diggin' ev'rythin'. On His headphones He's listening to Tex Mex rock'n'roll, blasting it into His holy head *so loud* that it ruffles the feathers of a passing angel. Into His head and out of His head, God *grooving*. Sitting there, reeling, *floating,* smitten by the wild accordions and Vox organs and guitars in full twangerama, this crazed Tex Mex motherfuckin' rock'n'roll, God makes a decision. He invents Joe King Carrasco and then smokes the mould.

A good day for God

October 30th 1993, Gaiety Theatre, Dublin

Kerrie Lee is *pushin'* Fiachna onto the stage - not that he's not hot to trot anyway - finds him a guitar and amp and tells him to just *go for it.*

The piano player, he's pumpin' the keys, proclaiming into the mike in his wild one gospellized countryboy rock'n'roll voice. The piano player, his ear cocks to the sound of another guitar. He looks round and his deep-set eyes take in Fiachna in his leather trousers in full twang. Fiachna, he catches the piano player's look and ... and the piano player, he grins, *diggin'* this new cat. Fiachna from Hothouse Flowers playin' with The Killer, whole lotta shakin' with Jerry Lee Lewis! Shit!

As Jerry Lee leaves the stage he passes Fiachna, turns back the few steps and puts the hand of

benediction on this Dublin whiteboy whose soul is steeped in black as much as Jerry Lee. Great balls of fuckin' fire! "You shake my nerves and you rattle my brain!"

Jerry Lee's the last one left, the last one still delinquent, the wildcat cat who cut 'Wild One' before Iggy and Bowie and lived it and often nearly died it. Elvis, Gene Vincent, Esquerita, the first crazed men of untamed rock'n'roll, they've gone to visit Old Shep in the sky. Little Richard, The Queen Of Rock'n'Roll, he left for the ministry before returning to the panstick. Chuck got busted by honky and did time for pubescent pussy. Priscilla? Myra? Johnny Cash, he can still hear that train a-comin', but Jerry Lee, he's out there on the borderline, marinated, more than still crazy after all these years. Jerry Lee: I love you.

April 3rd 1992, New Orleans

The Maple Leaf bar is jumpin'. Rockin' Dopsie is a *star*, his fire-engine red accordion pumpin', him tearin' into Big Joe Turner's 'Flip Flop And Fly' ("ah believe ah'm goin't' die"). David Rubin, one of Dopsie's sons in the band, he's screaming out Jesse Hill's revelationary message "Lemme tell you 'bout Ooh Pooh Pah Dooh!" Bono, he calls David "the Jimi Hendrix of the washboard".

Now Rockin' Dopsie stands there cool as a cucumber and he's telling you "Zydeco music done took over N'Awlins." He grins again. "David, he warm the band up for me so when I get up there for the crowd there's gonna be murder, I kill 'em ..."

What a perfect way to go ...

Rockin' Dopsie
Born: Lafayette, Louisiana "I was born in 1930 or 1932".
Died: En route to Opelousas, Louisiana August 26th 1993.

And the brothers and Clifton's sax man play on ...

April 19th 1992, San Francisco

It's Easter Sunday and earlier in the morning we'd gone to Glide Memorial, "the only church I feel completely at home in" as Bono describes it, the rockin' haven set up by the Rev. Cecil Williams for all of straight society's misfits: wild bikers, celebratory gays and lesbians, homeless, junkies, anyone. It's the only place where you can get an HIV test while the service is going on. Reverend Cecil, he is *shakin'*. And us benedictionary beneficiaries, we're clappin', dancin', steamin' as the drums kick and the guitar chops 'em out and the soul stirring voices of Jimmy Holmes and Waynette Runnels lead the choir, lead us all, in singin' "I feel better, I feel better, I feel better ..." Yo, God, baby! Going completely fuckin' bananas in the name of the Lord .....

And now in the late afternoon Bono and Edge, they're wandering around on the top of a cliff with the Golden Gate bridge far away in the background and Edge, he's talking about the Resurrection. "Jesus went to hell" he says all matter of fact. Jesus went to hell? Yes, after He died on the cross He went to hell. "It's in the bible" says Edge.

April 10th 1992, Tempe Arizona: Vote Elvis!

BP Fallon on Elvis: "Elvis is the key to America. He was brilliant and he didn't know why. And he kinda made a mess of it. Only difference is that America isn't dead."

You're on a mission. Tourists and students and U2 fans everywhere in the streets. Indian shops selling stuff where you can watch 'em make jewellery. Is this what it's come to, the great Indian tribes making tat for twats like you? At Chief Dodge on South Mill Avenue you buy delicately crafted silver earrings, little silver feathers with a tiny blue stone. Immediately lose one earring - thought you put it in your pocket or something. Aw what the heck - you only need one, anyways. Now then - where's the post office? Over there, um, sir. Ah yeah. You, you've never voted in America before. Right this second the choice is obvious. I mean, whadyawant, the Hillbilly Cat or the Elvis that's fat in his Donny Osmond suit? Huh? D'ya want sex or d'ya want blubber? *This* is democracy: choose your King (as long as it's Elvis). A big fat tick says slim is in. Gimme young Elvis, baby. Who wants a whale when you can have a wail? Scream for me, El ...

'Vote Baby'

'Vote Baby' is the child of 'Rock The Vote', the volunteer organisation committed to making it easier for Americans to vote ...

Son Of Sam - actually, Son Of Sam II, son of Uncle Sam - dressed in mock elegance in a $60 suit with the Stars and Stripes sewed onto it deliberately haphazardly by Helen Campbell in Wardrobe ... wearing a garish crucifix around his neck over a Marilyn Monroe tie ... Stars and Stripes sneakers on his feet ... announced on stage as 'The Future President of the United States' ... music: Alice Cooper and 'Elected', Gil Scott Heron and 'The Revolution Will Not Be Televised', Front 242 with 'Welcome To Paradise' and its demonstrative line "No sex before marriage" like a mad tele-evangelist from below the Cotton Curtain ... Bowie and 'Young Americans' with its line "Do you remember your President Nixon?" ...

Malcolm X 'No Sell-out' ...

'Vote Baby' badges Frisbeed into the audience, saying "It doesn't only affect Americans, this coming election, it's going to affect the whole world "... 'Rock The Vote' registration booths at the gigs ... Bono saying on stage "I hope you make the right choice because otherwise we're all fucked" ...

August 28th 1992, U2/Bill Clinton Radio Rabbit

Another evening in New York City on the Global Satellite Network: U2 from the radio studios of New York's Station WXRK, a coast to coast phone-in with the four members of the band taking calls from fans all over America ... **DJ:** "Here in New York live with all of the fellows in U2. Here on the Global Satellite Network we're going to go to the phones again and our next caller is named Bill. He's from Little Rock, Arkansas and he's listening to us in Magic 105. Hi Bill, how are you doing tonight?" **Bill:** "I'm fine, how are you? I can't believe I've got U2 on the phone. That's better than running for President. Are U2 there?" **Bono:** "This is Bono here. How do you want us to call you? Shall we call you Governor or Bill?" **Bill:** "No, you call me Bill." **Bono:** "Alright ... and you can call me Betty." *(Laughter from both ends of the phone)* **Bono:** "We don't suggest who people vote for but we do suggest that they vote." **Bill:** "Young people, people of 18 to 24, most of the millions of people listening to us tonight, they're listening because of you not because of me. And you don't need to ask them to vote for me, just ask them to look at the issues and *vote*. This 'Rock The Vote' thing you've been involved in is really, really good and I'm grateful to you for it."

Bono: "Well that's alright and I must say I think we've got to go now but I must say from all of us you *sound* like a President." **Bill:** "I want to say as a middle-aged man I appreciate the fact that you made 'The Joshua Tree' and that record 'Angel Of Harlem' in Sun Studios. You made me feel like I had a place in rock music even at 46." **Bono:** "Well Bill if we got you into it we must have got something wrong!" *(Laughter again from both ends of the telephones.)*

September 26th 1992, Ohio, President George Bush speaking in Bowling Green

"Governor Clinton doesn't think foreign policy's important but anyway he's trying to catch up. You may have seen this in the news; he was in Hollywood, seeking foreign policy advice from the rock drop, er-um, the rock group U2 ... You may not know this but they try to call me at The White House every night during the concert!

"But the next time we face a foreign policy crisis, I will work with John Major and Boris Yeltsin, and Bill Clinton can consult Boy George".

September 16th 1992, Ritz Carlton Hotel, Chicago

"I think there was drink involved" says Bono, scratching his head.

Bono: "It was in the Chicago two-level suite - same one - I got the party again in my room, arrived at about 2 in the morning having done a runner from Randell Stadium Wisconsin ..... There *was* drink involved and Fintan had banged up the blaster and there was a party going when *somebody* got it into their head - I don't know who it was - that Bill would like this, Bill would like to party. I *might* have said it actually, I might have said Bill would like a party, they're on the road, they're living the same life as us, they're travelling around blah blah blah. It was a joke. Someone said we'll call him up. Somebody took the notion seriously and went off to try and wake him up. Or to see if he was still awake. But Clinton's outer security guards monotoned 'No sir it is not possible I'm sorry sir now if you'd like to vacate this corridor now sir we'd appreciate your assistance sir I'm sorry sir'...

"But it wasn't *me*. I never left the room. I didn't even know they'd left the room. That's the last we heard of it. And I was off that night, I ended up in Edge's, we were working on a song for Sinatra -'Two Shots Of Happy, One Shot Of Sad'- at the piano. I ended up crashing in Edge's. Next morning there was a phone call. People were trying to trace where I was and they couldn't find me in my room. They needed me to go back to my room if I wanted to say hello to Bill - he had got the message that we had been looking for him the night before and said why didn't you wake me? 'I'll call around now' was his vibe, 'are they in?'"

Blinding daylight and bleary eyes and Bono still not quite together. He's still asleep really as he makes his fragile way back to his quarters. He looks just like what normal people think rock stars look like ... fucked. Clothes all crumpled, luggage eyes that an airline would charge overweight for, unshaven, tousled hair sticking out everywhere like the strands of a nightmare. Bono had hoped he would get back to his room before the great man would arrive for this summit, to try to pull himself together very quickly. "When I got there the surprise was that he was already in my room. Him and his people. No goons. Really good people, particularly a girl called Heather Beckel and a guy called George Stephanopoulos who is one of the smartest guys in the whole of the Clinton camp, and who I think was the guy that turned them on to U2. I don't mean that makes him smart but he is a very young guy, cool guy, he's about our age, 32-33. I don't know what his gig is at the moment. I think he was the spokesperson for Bill Clinton, still is.

"We seemed to get on. Larry asked Clinton why he would want to be President. He said 'Good question, 'cos sometimes even I wonder, sometimes I marvel how *difficult* it's going to be to change things, but if the President of the United States can't change things, no one can.' That was the vibe.

"I asked him about Irish access visas, the fact that Ireland's supposed to have a special relationship with America but we need special visas whereas the UK doesn't. Then we talked about what George Lucas was doing with computers, developing an interactive computer system for the schools to educate America and I thought that maybe it would be worth checking out what George Lucas is doing and he said he was already aware of it. And we talked music, saxophone, and then there was this thing that the nickname by his aides for him was Elvis.

"And the odd thing was *he* was essentially on tour and what brought two very disparate entities together was the touring life - he was on the road too ..."

August 1993, Salman Rushdie: London, Dublin and Bono and Ali's house

After the first Wembley show, the Pet Shop Boys visit dressed in cowls. Roger Daltrey, still ringleted and almost looking like the geezer who used to sing with The Who, banters with Larry who is sitting on the corner of a table. Salman Rushdie, he's here too. A couple of guys at the door with eyes that keep moving in all directions stand twitchy testament to Mr Rushdie's presence.

Earlier, MacPhisto had phoned the author of 'Satanic Verses', he with the fatwah on his head, live from stage only to have Salman stroll on with his mobile phone and be greeted with a tidal wave of applause from the 72,000 audience. Wow! "I'm not frightened of men with horns" Salman informed the multitude, smiling lopsidedly.

Now it's Dublin after the last Zooropa show and that other Satanic Majesty Mick Jagger is hanging out, twitching from one side of the room to the other. He's not at all like the Widow Twankey panto figure of 'Steel Wheels', looking amazingly well like he's just finished filming 'Performance'. Mick the voodoo queen lounge lizard darts around. Jerry Hall, she's tossing her mane of hair and laughing Miss Texas style, Yasmin Le Bon tending her child asleep on a sofa. Naomi. Christy. Gavin and René, natch. Bob Geldof and Paula. In the tent after the gig.

The previous night Geldof was headed off, couldn't wait to leave. "I was right Beep wasn't I?" "Well it wasn't the greatest show tonight, Bob". "It was expensive bollox signifying fuck all. I didn't fuckin' *feel* anything." Bob, he says he'll be back tomorrow, bringing Paula, "but I'll only be staying for ten minutes." And now Bob Geldof is in the hospitality tent, enthusing about tonight's blast of Zoo TV. "It *was* good" he concedes. "Really good. Now I know what you were on about in Russia. Really good ..."

The Editor of Musician Magazine, Bill Flanagan, fair play to him, wants his picie taken with Salman. Yeah, a Salman picie would be a good vibe. "Hey, hey" you're going as Salman and pals break up from their Bill Flanagan line-up.

"You missed your chance, Beep. You're too late" teases Bono.

"I'm never too late, baby." And Salman and Yasmin almost and Christy and King B, his head tilted back, grinning, a Bill Haley kisscurl, do their camera thing. Warm, baby.

And you're talking to Salman Rushdie ("Oh yes, you took my photograph" he offers as recognition) and you say, subtle as ever "Look, this is a direct question but don't you ever just shit yourself?".

"Well" says Salman all sage-like, "you get used to it ..."

And why do you like U2? "Because they take chances, they take risks and they're not afraid of falling flat on their face. They're committed and you have to admire that."

And then it reverts to more import matters like how do you travel on planes?

"That's not something I feel would be wise to discuss" Salman says.

Geldof's been ear-wigging the verbal and now he jumps in with "At airports, do you just go up to the desk and say 'Salman Rushdie'?" "No. It doesn't work like that." **BP:** "What was it like going on stage at Wembley. Was it frightening?" **Salman:** "No, no. With 72,000 people applauding you, this rush of warmth, you can't feel anything but good. And I didn't even have to sing!"

Salman, he's changing the subject. "And what are you up to now, Mr Geldof?"

Geldof, he's off to Leeds Castle tomorrow to see a performance by his pal Pavarotti. "A great geezer" says Bob. "It hasn't changed at all with me" Bob is saying all self-mocking and digging it too, "it's still all one big lig!"

And the next day, at Bono and Ali's ... Sunday afternoon, day after the last Zooropa gig ... it's getting to be late afternoon now. We're on the tennis court under a huge marquee that contains groups of tables and chitter-chat and lunch is winding down. Salman Rushdie is at the McGuinness table. Jim Sheridan is sitting with his wife Fran near Chris Blackwell and Mary. Patsy Kensit and hubby Jim Kerr. Joe O'Herlihy and Marian. Bob and Gretchen Koch. Dennis and Lyndsey Sheehan. Dave and Ursula Fanning. Steve and Maria Averill. Wim and Donata Wenders. Tom Freston and Judy McGrath from MTV. Jann Wenner and Jane from Rolling Stone. Larry and Ann, Adam and Naomi, Edge and Morleigh ... and Bono and Ali, natch. Yasmin Le Bon looks completely beautiful and vulnerable.

Earlier that afternoon ... Salman Rushdie is standing alone, standing alone outside of the marquee and his bespectacled eyes are peering through the object a couple of feet from his face: the tennis court fence. Only a tennis court fence, yes, but still a boundary. Still a barrier. And never a shield. Salman Rushdie gazes through the wire fence out at the sea, the waves frothing before they hit the beach. Behind the wire fence and through it Salman Rushdie looks out ....

June 20th 1992, Manchester G MEX Hall - Stop Sellafield Gig

You're folding your Elvis cloak in front of the band's dressing-room when Paul comes into this backstage area asking where the loo is. "There" you go, pointing. "Where?" says Paul. "There" you point again, indicating the little steps that lead into the mobile toilet. "Where?" says Paul. "What exactly are you looking for, Paul?" you say. "Lou Reed" Paul says.

U2 are heading this Greenpeace bill with Kraftwerk, B.A.D. II, King Boogaloo and Public Enemy, the first time they've played with Public Enemy. And Lou Reed makes a surprise appearance during his song 'Satellite Of Love'. And the concert is to protest the Sellafield Nuclear Plant which is going to be the biggest in Europe and getting bigger. Bono's wife Ali is involved in Greanpeace and they're trying to do something about it. After the show the band slip off without explanation in a bus and to do some Greenpeace action which nobody is supposed to know about. A week previously in Kiel in Germany Bono was already agitated. And now four days before the Sellafield Concert, Bono's standing in the corner of the Sheffield Arena and U2 haven't even gone on stage and he's worn out. Lawyers all day. You put the plot together and you're ready to read the newspapers the next day.

As Adam and yourself trudge back towards the coach over the deserted beach, it's spooky, very very spooky. By now the sun is up and it's a glorious Sunday by the seaside yet the beach - apart from us loonies wandering around looking like the long lost children of a Michelin tyre, enormous human-sized sperms - this gorgeous sandy beach remains completely deserted. Golden sands, a picture postcard frozen in fear. At the carpark, families play, little children allowed as far as the small stone wall that divides dry land from the dangerous grains of sand. In the background, the warped nuclear towers vomit out dark threatening clouds that fill the sky with a vile pungent unstated fear. Adam remarks on the group of policemen he notices are taking photographs of us from half a mile away. "They were using poxy little cameras and using flash" chortles Adam. "None of their pictures will come out! Why don't they just buy tomorrow's papers if they really want to know who's here ..."

As we climb back on the coach, weary, dazed, someone points out to Bono that his cowboy boots are *dangerous*, having trod in radiated sand. Reluctantly, *dutifully*, he pulls them off and throws them in a bin. As the coach is pulling out we spy some fans retrieving the radiated boots from out of the trash can. Rapid negotiations ensue with the bewildered fans finally swapping the atomic boots for autographs.

It is a lovely Sunday sunny day. The Windscale village is olde worlde, old stone buildings. The unarrested coach speeds back to Manchester. Annie Nightingale and Nikki Sudden are doing zzzs as through the panoramic windows those left with any perception of the outside world gawk and point at the police roadblocks only now being set up. "A bit late, chaps" Bono mouths.

BP: "The British government tried to prohibit you, didn't they?"

Bono: "There was an injunction taken out. We were going to turn up at the *door* by road, which would've been the right way to do it - but they wouldn't let us, they cut off the roads with police cordons. They injuncted us and threatened to seize our assets, *and* Greenpeace's assets and they basically *bullied* us or attempted to bully us from not showing up. So we showed up. We came by sea and they *couldn't* stop us because in England, thank God, the beach is still public property up to the high tide line. So we brought our barrels and left them on the high tide line to the embarrassment of the authorities and British Nuclear Fuels. So it was a *great* day for Ireland! And England!"

May 31st 1992, Earl's Court Arena, London

You and your posse - Patsy, your sister Patricia, Rovena Cardiel, Martha Henley, Melanie Williams, Joan Ewen - are strolling through the echoey canyons of Earls Court Arena, headed back to your dressing room when you see Edge, who's leaving. "Sinéad's looking for you" Edge says.

You find her in the band's hospitality area, where there's Kirsty MacColl and Steve Lillywhite and Chrissie Hynde and Peter Gabriel and, his Zapata moustache in full bloom and having a little snooze in his chair, Shane MacGowan.

Sinéad, she's over in a corner having a heart-to-heart with Bono. They haven't spoken to each other for years, ever since Sinéad let loose an explosion of vitriol against U2 in the media, calling them insincere and manipulative and full of bullshit - often through your own pages in the Sunday Tribune in Ireland.

The next day you tell Bono it was brilliant seeing him'n'Sinéad together. "That was surreal" Bono chuckles.

In Gothenburg you're saying to Bono "I've been thinking about you saying that meeting up again with Sinéad was surreal. It wasn't surreal at all. It was beautiful, two folk mending bridges, loving each other, being friends again."

"No, no," Bono smiles, "it's not that that was surreal. The surreal thing was you taking pictures of all this going on ..."

WALLS & BRIDGES

live Goldfish

In the chilly wee hours of morning Edge and King Boogaloo emerge from Wanda's bar in Montreal on Maisonneuve West, this palace of flesh Wanda's where ladies clad only in high-heeled shoes and hi-fi suntan mingle with the clientele. Well, they don't exactly **mingle**. They come up to your table and kneel on a little footstool. They kinda ... well, they, uh, fondle themselves while you don't know **where** to put your eyes. And of course, you're not allowed to **touch**. Yourself, you get the impression that Edge isn't entirely used to finding himself in places like Wanda's.

Climbing into his waiting limo Edge is spotted by a wandering tribe of U2 fans from across the border. Americans. One in particular is even more thrilled than is usual to meet his guitar icon. "Hey man" he gushes at his hero, "I got tickets to see you guys last night by winning a competition on a radio station." Turns out our enthusiastic new dawn acquaintance, he'd gotten his seats for the U2 concert at The Forum here in Montreal last night by eating more live goldfish than any other competitor. His nearest rival only managed to gulp a measly one hundred and four. Our new champion swallowed one hundred and six live goldfish.

Edge is impressed, amazed, confused, disgusted, bewildered. Later on he says the very thought of all those poor wriggling goldfish in this person's stomach made him feel somewhat queasy. Edge, now a look of uncertain astonishment on his face, asks the goldfish guy what did he do after he'd swallowed these unfortunate creatures. "Me?" the guy says with an aw-shucks look to his face. "Me? I went out and had me some beers and a pizza."

There are magazines, newspapers, faxes of reviews and a crushed rose trampled into the carpet. Rolling Stone describes this madness on which we find ourselves as "the Irish band's magical mystery tour of the 90's ... total sensory overload."

USA Today in its cover story is headlining the Zoo TV Tour as "A Flashy New Shout At The Global Village" going on to depict "the group's dazzling road show, complete with its own satellite TV

that phone lines broke down completely. A certain Ms Joanne Waddel, a New England telephone manager, is quoted in the Boston paper as saying "We expected a lot of calls but this was unbelievable. It was complete gridlock. I don't know how else to describe it. They bombed us right out of the water."

And here's Larry Moulter, president of Boston Garden giving his fifty dollars' worth: "The demand was overwhelming. I heard there were half a million calls in the first hour." Huh! In Atlanta, anxious ticket seekers

His nearest rival only managed to gulp a measly 104

live Goldfish

broadcast system ... featuring a trippy and decadent concert of the dazzling visuals and adventurous music". Bono is quoted as saying "We can beam concerts into Peking or Prague for free. We can spawn video bootlegs in cultures where it's hard to get our music. That's exciting. Rock'n'roll is about being untamed sexually, spiritually, politically. That's why in some cultures it's still a threat".

Bono ... at every gig mixing Las Vegas trash and flash with soulful emotion, a cauldron of humour, sex and passion. The humour, natch, is often self-deprecating. As Rolling Stone notes, referring to the Fly becoming the Messiah Of Madness in a mirrored silver suit, "He enters in leather and leaves in glitter."

At the opening concert in Lakeland, Florida, all tickets were sold out in four minutes. It's a pattern that's repeating everywhere. In Boston, such was the demand

March 24th 1992, press buzz and broken phones

logged more than *two* million calls.

Today's Montreal Gazette in its front page review of last night's wild concert here at The Forum reports "The Zoo TV tour hits Montreal with 20-odd TV and video screens flashing images at synapse-snapping speed ... Bono's performance, part camp and all drunken rock'n'roll passion, made mockery of the band's holier-than-thou image - and loosed complete abandon in a sold-out building. The crowd's reaction, from Bono's lurching entrance to his encore singing 'Desire' in silver lamé, carrying a full-length mirror, was easily the loudest in Forum history". Describing the gig as "party decadence and serious rock'n'roll" the piece goes on to report "Bono was utterly, perfectly graceless and the band, playing to a crowd that had obviously lost itself, was pure muscle."

Muscle of love, baby.

Road Crew, Trabbies and Riggers in Drag

The road crew are the unsung heroes of the tour so this is a warble for them. Longest-serving of the U2 team - the U2 family - is Joe O'Herlihy, Cork man, soundman and sound man. Assisted by Robbie Adams and Joe Ravitch, it is Joe who ensures that even the most difficult venue can have amazing sound. After a concert in California, Joe is in the band's dressing room standing both humble and proud while Bono beams and Quincy Jones tells Joe the man from Cork that "Tonight was the best live sound I've *ever* heard". In Vegas before the encore Joe darts from his mixing desk past Peter Buck from REM and whacks his arm around Irish showband superstar Brendan Bowyer, 'Ireland's original Elvis'. "Take a pic" Joe urges, delighted to meet the singer from The Royal Showband, Waterford. 'Do The Hucklebuck', baby.

There's Billy Louthe, red-haired and very Irish and living in Philadelphia, who helps maintain your silver-mirrored open-topped Trabbie. At one point, every time you play a bass-heavy CD - Public Enemy, The Brand New Heavies, Sly And The Family Stone doin' 'Don't Call Me Nigger Whitie' - zzzt, zzzt, zzzt, the damn CD player would skip'n'jump. Enter Billy checkin' the four CD players built into your four-wheeled disco ... and Joe with Robbie Adams and Joe Ravitch from his stand in the middle of the arena or stadium does some magic O'Herlihy tweak on his sound and everything is hunky-dory.

The Trabants, they're wild. *Your* silver machine, lining the seats is cool yellow leopardskin courtesy of Adele Hocking. There's another Trabbie wrapped in fake orange leopardskin, something like that, and covered in spikes all vicious and threatening like a mind-warped escapee from 'Mad Max IX'. And during 'Bullet The Blue Sky', from its perverse metal swan's neck, it aims downwards onto the stage, onto the band, onto the audience, into their heads, lights shining like evil searchlights probing the brightness of their minds as Edge's boom-on-the-head guitar strafes the heads off the audience, as zapping as Zeppelin.

Another Trabbie is painted by Cathy Owens, the Dublin artist with more balls than a pool game. The message across it is a Want Ad from Cyberspace. It reads "Conservative Cyberpunk Doctor, SWM 26, seeks SWF or SAF for weird and exciting adventures. I'm into surveillance and high-tec mayhem. You - a savage aggressor or sultry vixen looking for a partner in crime. Tall a + (I'm 6'4") Box 7126."

In Paris, Jake Kennedy, the ex-school teacher who worked with U2 way back when and then left and is now back again, back as Deputy Production Manager, Jake runs into your dressing room to demand if you're ready. "You gotta go on now, Beep, Fatima Mansions' set only ran for twenty minutes". Afterwards, unnecessarily, he apologizes for hustling you. In Tempe Arizona, Rocco the Assistant Tour Manager slams into the Portacabin you're sharing with The Sugarcubes, tears into your room where you're dancing around in your knickers and sox to Stevie Wonder on your blaster singin' his MLK tribute song 'Happy Birthday'. "Put some clothes on quickly" Rocco fires at you. "Public Enemy have left the stage after one song." "Help me with my cloak" you say.

Flying Saucers catering, they're **brilliant**. Helen Findley is your guarding angel, always ready with something amazing that even a complete crank like you can eat. And on the MGM Grand, Mary Fleming always has brown rice or something for you to chow down on.

The riggers, sometimes after a gig they'll open their club 'The Riggers Arms', the riggers crowned in full regalia serving behind the bar. They throw a great one in Boston Foxboro Stadium. At another, the band perform their barman duty dispensing drinks to their workmates. The riggers, they're great morale boosters for Zoo whenever it needs a kick up the arse.

November 5th 1992, The Ritz Carlton, San Francisco

It's Dennis's birthday today. Earlier, he'd said he didn't want the usual big deal, everyone gettin' together for a huge dinner. "I don't feel right" Dennis declared, "with someone spending a couple of grand on a meal for my birthday. I'd really like the money to go to an Aids charity."

Visitations: Zooropa '93

For the Zooropa '93 Tour Paul Oakenfold is the disc jockey, a truly talented remixer who started off with Happy Mondays and ended up doin' wild U2 remixes of 'Real Thing', 'Mysterious Ways', 'Crashed Car', 'Numb' and his classic teeth-rattler 'Lemon' along the way. Paul, he's understated and underspoken, a genuine grin on his face and often assisted by Colin Hudd.

Tim Ross and Darrel Ives from security are gone and in their places are Eric Haush who's quietly comic and very cool and Scott Nichols, the guy all the models are after and who looks like Fabian in the 50's.

Ellen Darst is working for Electra Records with Keryn Kaplan now runnin' the New York office.

And every time you now visit the Zoo, you don't even have your *own* dressing room any more. Life's really tuff like that, sometimes.

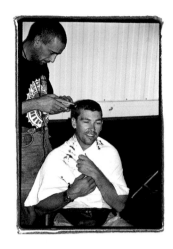

the crew

Bono on the Riggers:

"**The riggers are often doing their loadouts in drag, or at least one piece of drag, eyeliner or lipstick. And these are very straight men, let me tell you, and the idea of them in dresses shifting the 150 tons of Zoo TV out of venues onto trucks has given us all some laughter. The riggers are the sexiest men on the tour - just ask the women folk around us!**"

Xmas 1992: four days in Dublin from South Beach Miami, seeing your sister Patricia and your brother Peter and his wife Jean, seein' your nephew Adam and your new niece Alice, seeing the band and Paul and Ossie at the party at Edge's house, seeing Sinéad at her father's place where she's staying, only gettin' time to talk to Fiachna on the phone ... Then

The Dead Boys' 'Sonic Reducer', Eddie Vedder dissing the Marky Mark posters up in Times Square ..... Keef and his cohorts blowing it wild, the angel of perdition sprung to have wings, Keef the ballerina of rock'n'roll pose, goat's head group that build up, Bobby Keyes' horn roaring, twist'n'turn and then stop splat! on a mini-note. What an *amazing* band!

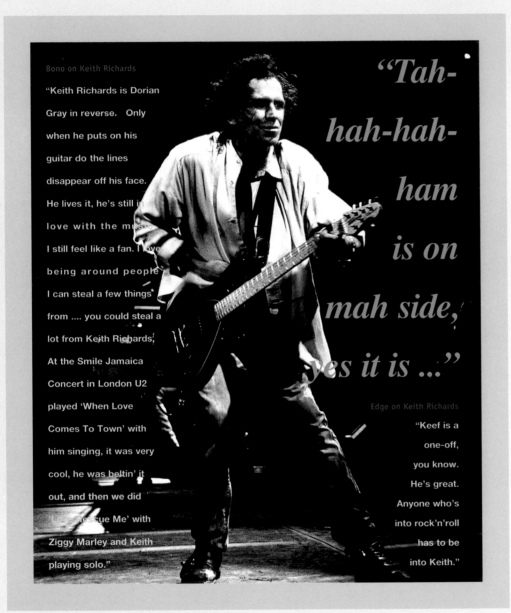

Bono on Keith Richards

"Keith Richards is Dorian Gray in reverse. Only when he puts on his guitar do the lines disappear off his face. He lives it, he's still in love with the music, I still feel like a fan. I love being around people I can steal a few things from .... you could steal a lot from Keith Richards. At the Smile Jamaica Concert in London U2 played 'When Love Comes To Town' with him singing, it was very cool, he was beltin' it out, and then we did 'Rescue Me' with Ziggy Marley and Keith playing solo."

"Tah-hah-hah-ham is on mah side, yes it is ..."

Edge on Keith Richards

"Keef is a one-off, you know. He's great. Anyone who's into rock'n'roll has to be into Keith."

Christmas 1992, Dublin and New Year 1993, NYC

New York City New Year's Eve, King Boogaloo - aided by his technical guru, Hiphoprisy's Vaughn Martinian - doin' the sounds and the vibes at this ol' dancehall The Academy off Times Square, Boogaloo on a bill with Keef Richards and his X-pensive Winos and - yo! - Pearl Jam, live across the US of A on ABC TV.

Pearl Jam, revving up through

And Sarah Dash she of Pattie LaBelle And The Bluebells supportin' The Stones way back when on American treks when Keith was the guitar player with the stick-out ears and the goofy expression ..... And Brian was the cool one, luggage eyes and a vanity-laden blond fringe that shrouded doubt and paranoia and a music genius. And Jagger, prissy, petulant, child-bearing lips, "you ask my, to give up the hand of the gurl ah lurve ..." Jagger'd do his James Brown and the girls, they'd wet themselves. Brian had just to grin the grin of the golden devil and the girls ... they'd **come**. And Keith became Keef, and Keef learned, learned it his way.

And now Pearl Jam and Robert Cray have joined Keef an' co and they're tearing through the Don Nix song that Freddie King, bless him, that Freddie almost took to heaven. Keef 'n' Eddie Vedder, they're roaring it out, voices bouncing off each other, singin' "Goin' down, down, down, down, down ..."

Which way is up, baby?!

Rewind: Still at The Academy, Keef's strokin' his

Fender and his left knee's up in the air and his left foot is dancing, and his ragged glory face transforms itself into some pallored **glow**, the man taken by the music, and his lips crack open and his eyes are shining, shining, and you can see that he's been in a million shipwrecks and survived, and now Keith Richards is sharing the vocals with Sarah Dash, and the lost and lonesome voice that sang George Jones's 'Apartment No 9' in the storm that was Toronto ... that voice, it's now gargled with N'Awlins r'n'b, a splash of Jamaican roots, mon ... and English rude boy, celebrating freedom and joy, singing "Tah-hah-hah-ham is on mah side, yes it is ..."

Yeah, 'Happy' New Year.

You're in California staying with your Silverheaded Blondied Iggied pal Nigel Harrison.

You're at the 'Rock For Choice' freedom for abortion concert in LA at The Palladium - the concert partly organized by the all-girl group L7 - having volunteered to do interviews for ABC TV's 'In Concert' series. It's a great snappin' lineup: Green Apple Quickstep - Tai, he's a **real** one - Eddie Vedder doin' a solo acoustic set, Seven Year Bitch, Concrete Blonde doin' **their** acoustic thang, Holy Water, Mary's Danish, Screaming Trees, Rage Against The Machine.

Dave Pirner comes by to lend support, having just sung with Soul Asylum at the Universal Amphitheatre

where they were giggin' with Keith Richards and his X-pensive Winos. Also adding their voices to the Pro Choice campaign, here tonight talking to MTV and ABC, are Neneh Cherry and Michael Stipe. Just recently, Michael and his REM buddy Mike Mills had joined up with Adam and Larry to play 'One' at President Clinton's MTV Inaugural Ball. Adam and Larry, they'd met up with the two Michaels the night before in a bar, and just went for it. This once-off group, they called themselves Automatic Baby.

"Adam really enjoyed the thing you guys did at Clinton's Inaugural Ball" you remark to Michael Stipe.

"Adam who?" he says deadpanning ...

January 23rd 1993, Los Angeles

Adam sitting there in his 'I Like To Watch' t-shirt that Fintan got for him and he's just finished his last phone interview. "Yes, we will be taking a short break and then we'll be playing in Europe again, and yes the stadiums like we're doing here" and "Yes well Bono does write the lyrics but no ... that's not to say some of the songs weren't entirely unaffected by Edge's marital situation" blah blah blah are answers you hear Adam politely giving for the zillionth time as you gawk into the early evening out of Adam's suite. Down on the ground in the dusk you can make out Edge and Dennis playing tennis. It's weird watching them, almost voyeuristic. Like you're looking through a telescope backwards. Adam joins you at the window. "You can see Dennis, he's determined to win" he chuckles. **"I must confess I don't have anything planned for tonight"** Adam confesses. He's such an old British gent sometimes. You can see him in the Punjab sixty years ago knocking back the gins and tracing the air with his cigarette like an upper class drag queen. "What are you doing?" he asks you again. "I'll check out the vibe" King Boogaloo sprouts up. Boogaloo, he goes down to the lobby to ask where the action is. King Boogaloo's mind, it wanders into some sort of thought process. "I haven't quite figured out why these guys have me on tour. I mean, I know I'm the DJ and can turn them on to a few good sounds and I *really love* doin' it but I have a feeling it's something more devious ... *They* know that I know the baddest parts of all these towns ... 'cause I've been there before. No better man for getting offside." And getting offside can be a very dicey operation. *These* kinda hotels - chandeliers a go go, marble all over the place, concierges who would call you "Sir" however obnoxious you might be - *these* kinda hotels aren't going to be too keen to direct their valued clientele to the nearest sleaze pit where everybody takes drugs and men dress up as women and where the music is *pumpin'*. Which is where you want to go, normally. Or at least somewhere that's *kickin'*. If you aren't careful they can send you to some fuckin' oo la la joint where everything's plastic - and that's just the surgery. By now Adam's in the lobby too, clad in a very fetching dress. Well, no, it's more like some sort of sari that he picked up on his travels. The concierge reels off a list of names like Mirabelle's and Longfellows. They all sound very false-eyelashy and maybe even lacquer. "Then, err, there's The Bridge Club". The concierge clears his throat. "But you might not want to go there ...". A red flag to a bulldozer. Concierge notices our potential enthusiasm. "It's a 60-40 club, sir". What's that? "Well sir, it's about sixty percent gay and forty percent straight". "Would you be kind enough to tell the driver the address?" "Certainly sir". Our cab, it has a sign inside that says 'Ban Guns And You Kill Freedom'. There's the smell of stale sex in the back seat.

The Bridge Club. Get in line, show ID - Zoo TV laminates get you into *The Pope*, if you want. *Adam* gets you into *God*, if that's your poison. "Oh, this way sir, you're very welcome, havva good time", mingle, guy comes up "Wow I saw you in 19 blah blah", arms like a disintegrating windmill, eyes all wide like volcanoes are going to rush out of them, a manic grin that's a spit away from dribble. Adam just nods, a mixture of natural politeness and suffering tolerance, smiles and says "Maybe we should go over there, Beep". Adam moves away. You're left alone with a joint in the car park. Folk necking at the club's entrance. What a gas. Back inside: get given a little side room, I guess the place where the club stores the beer. Crates of the stuff around. Two girls. Jazz Woodbine ...

Rabbit from beyond the stratosphere

BP: **"What have you learnt out of all this U2ism? What are your words of wisdom to the masses?"** Adam: **"It was great fun."** BP: **"And is it thus frightening?"** Adam: **"I think that's good for you though."** BP: **"And have you ever fallen over, over the cliff-edge?"** Adam: **"I kind-a bounce off either side of it from time to time."** BP: **"Adam Clayton, what is more important: the sun or the moon?"** Adam: **"The sun. Because it brings life and a new day."**

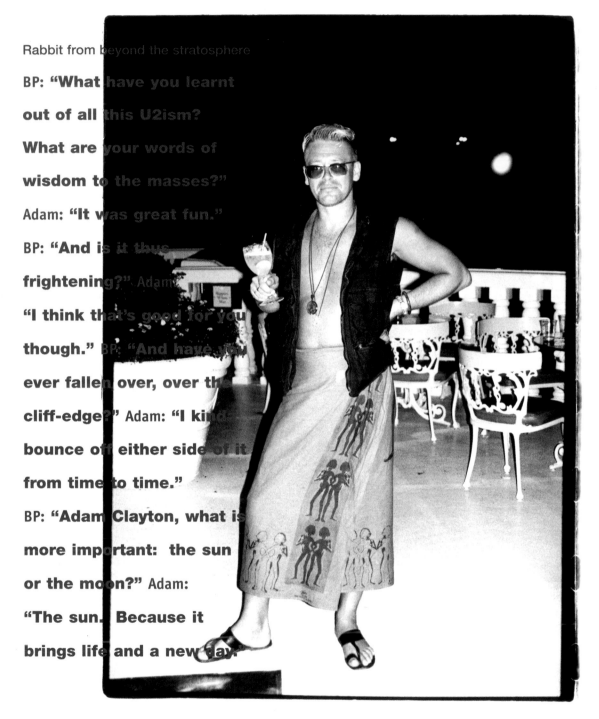

MADAMIMADAM

February 18th 1992, Dublin to New York

Before the great rendezvous of the Zoo TV army in Lakeland Florida for another week and more of intensive rehearsals, Adam sets off to America ahead of the band. Adam, he's gone via New York to visit the Aids activist and artist David Wojnarowicz - best known to U2 fans for his striking 'One' image which depicts buffalo plummeting over a cliff to their doom, this emotive image which forms the cover of the single. "Smell the flowers while you can". Yes. David Wojnarowicz is dying of Aids. "It'll probably be my last chance to see him" Adam says. It is.

October 26th 1992, Sunset Marquis, West Hollywood

Flashback: Dublin Christmas '78 and you're at this party thrown by Charles O'Connor, the guitarist in Horslips. A young chap comes up to you, thrusting the demo tape by his group into your hands. Another bloody demo tape. And then this guy, glasses, permed frizzy blond hair like a bleached Jimi Hendrix, he starts pumping you, asking you all these questions about the music business. Really good incise precise questions. This guy

is brimming intent. In rock'n'roll, attitude is as important as musical skill, the sense of going for it.

This probing young man has gotten you curious. Produced by Horslips' Barry Devlin, the tape's got something. The rhythm section is stiff, the singer's a bit all over the place but the songs ... they're vibrant with the freshness of punk yet kinda different ... And there's one track you particularly like, 'Shadows And Tall Trees'. And the guitaring - it glistens and shimmers, echoes of Tom Verlaine from Television and with the consistency of mercury like Barry Melton with Country Joe And The Fish yonks ago in radical hippie dippie Berkeley. The bass player, that's who gave you the tape. His phone number is on the cassette case along with his name, Adam, and the name of his group: U2. *This* is your introduction.

And now ... West Hollywood, October '92, fourteen years later. In your suite Adam is talking about the very first day Bono, Edge, Dik, Adam and Larry got together at Mount Temple school. "We didn't have much equipment so we pooled what we had. There was Larry's first drum kit which was kinda a toy thing, Edge and his brother Dik had made an electric guitar out of a piece of wood, and I had a bass and I think a speaker. And I had an

amp. We plugged everything into the amp, we got an old microphone from a tape recorder and just made an awful noise. It was a random banging and clatter and strumming that bore no resemblance to anything else you've ever heard. But it was fun!" BP: "Were you dreadful as a band?" Adam: "That would be a kinda compliment, I wouldn't say dreadful was even close."

As well as supplying wobbly bass-playing to this altogether untogether cacophonous combo, Adam the schoolboy rebel in his hippie Afghan coat impressed with words like 'gig' as if he knew what he was talking about. "There was this undeniable belief" Edge recalls, "that Adam instilled in us. We only wanted to play music, we didn't think about it in terms of making money or making records but Adam always did. And Adam was our first manager." This new group's driving force even suggested that they should get themselves on television. "We looked at him as if he was out of his mind" Edge says today at Adam's audaciousness. U2 got their television spot.

Much of his early life was spent in Kenya, where his father was an airline pilot. Adam's younger brother Sebastian is also a bass player, having played with Moby Dick. Adam's sister Cindy who's great gas lives in London. Adam's British upper-crust accent - he's now an Irish citizen - can be interpreted as pompous, hiding a truly gentle heart.

Adam has always been regarded as the rock'n'roll renegade of U2 and, for those who in the past have denounced U2 as some sort of musical detergent, hope was always found in Adam's public misadventures.

Adam's the one who comes by your quarters to hang the most, to listen to sounds - today we're vibing to Pharcyde and Jah Wobbles's CD 'Rising Above Bedlam' with Sinéad warbling 'Visions Of You'. An' Marc playing acoustic live on KDAY here in groovy El Lay a hundred years ago. Some Otis. George Clinton 'Free Your Mind' ("an' yo ass will follow. The kingdom of heaven is within." Thanx, Big George). Stuff .....

Sitting here at the Sunset Marquis you ask Adam your chum "If a Martian landed and was introduced to you and asked you what do you do, what would you say?" Quicker than the shake of a lamb's tail comes the reply "I simulate love-making by beating a piece of wood with a metal wire on which it vibrates."

Good vibrations, baby ...

BP: WHAT WOULD YOU LIKE TO HAVE THAT YOU DON'T?

Edge: A clone. A clone with good timing so I could send him off to do the things th

xtract from the BP U2 Q&A, Zoo TV tour programme volume 1, recorded jan. 1992

"Where's Larry?" says Bono. "He's gone already" says Edge. Bono, Edge, Adam and Naomi are sitting in the bar of the Hotel Majestic Roma. Adam and Naomi, they look like they haven't slept too much.

The call comes for Bono, Edge and Adam to board the coach that is taking them to Naples for the gig tomorrow night. Bret Alexander appears, his child in a buggy, and asks us would we mind keeping an eye on the infant. "When Adam and I announced that we were getting married" Naomi says, "because it was so quickly and so sudden, so soon after we'd met, all my girlfriends said 'Are you pregnant?'"

You look at Naomi. "No, no I'm not!" she giggles, blagging a ciggie from you. You hardly know this person, hardly know her at all, but the very first time you met her you took to her immediately.

"Quincy Jones sent me that programme you did" Naomi's now remarking, referring to the first BP U2 Q&A you'd done at the very beginning of 1992 for the Zoo TV tour programme where you'd asked all the band all the same questions without each of them knowing how the others had responded. To the question "What would you like to have that you don't?" Adam had replied quick as a flash "Naomi Campbell". 'Course, Adam and Naomi hadn't met then. 'Twas to be a year and more before their paths crossed.

July 8th 1993, Hotel Majestic Roma

Naomi relates the story. "I was going to New York on Concorde to do a job and I'm always missing planes so I had to take the next one. Bono was on the plane and he said 'Why don't you come to this party' - it was the farewell party for Ellen Darst - so I went and everyone was saying 'Why don't you go over and talk to Adam?' Adam was sitting there and he looked so shy ...

"Anyway, I was on another plane back to London and Adam was on it and we sat together and it just ... **happened** ..."

And now, naturally, you're talking about music. Naomi, for all her tender years, knows **tons** about music. "I went to the Rock'n'Roll Hall Of Fame awards with Eric and Cream played, Eric, Jack and Ginger. It was **fantastic**. The Doors played with Eddie Vedder singing which was really good, and Etta James was ... God, she's got an amazing voice. But the best thing was Sly And The Family Stone. They sang, just sang a cappella, and it was beautiful, so moving ..." She puffs at her ciggie.

"Y'know," says Naomi, her musical verbal slowing down as she loses herself in her thoughts, "y'know at the beginning of this year I told my mother that this year there was **no way** I was going to get involved in another relationship. It's funny the way things work out, isn't it?"

Yes.

Adam: Naomi Campbell

I can't do. **Larry:** I would like to play guitar. **Bono:** Feet. My legs just seem to end.

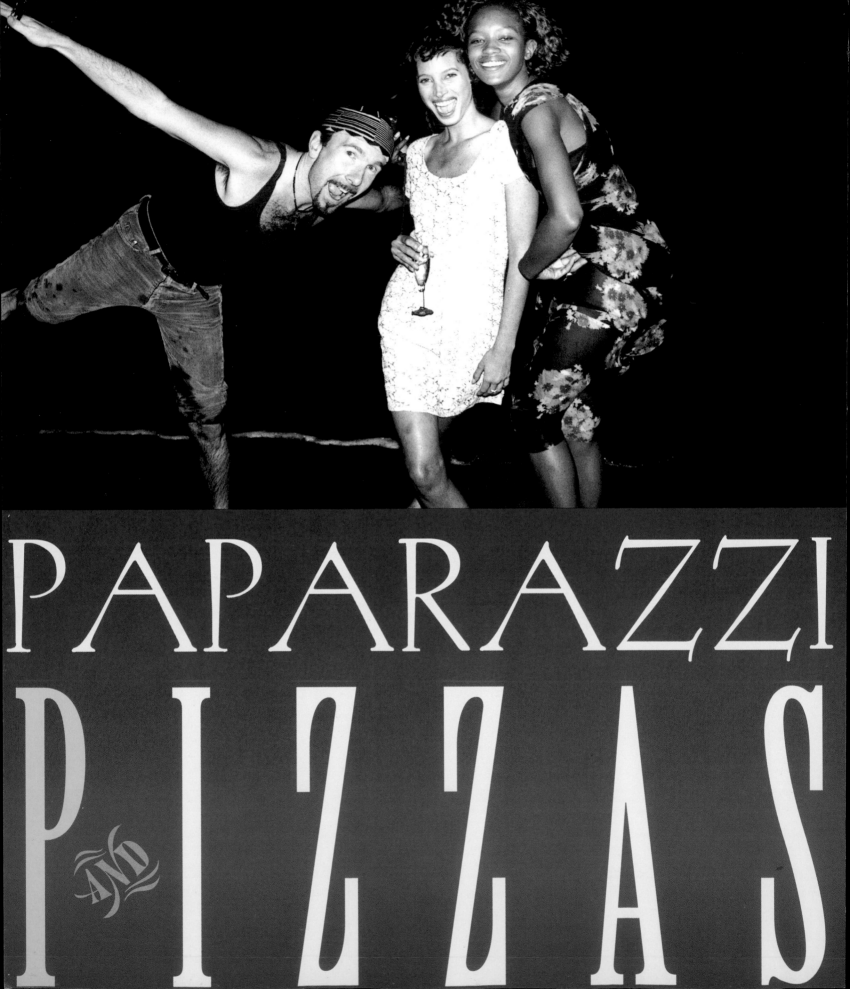

PAPARAZZI

PIZZAS

AND

You're speeding down the highway back to Rome. It's, what, four in the morning and you're in this big coach, the band and Naomi and Christy Turlington and Claire and Jeff Ament and Eddie Vedder and Beth, Eddie's girlfriend from nine years.

"I need a piss" you announce.

"So do I" says Larry.

"So do I" says Naomi.

Earlier ... vroom! vroom! vroom! exit out of the Stadio Flaminio where some bastard during the gig stole your Malcolm X jacket, a camera lens and a pair of glasses. There's a police car in front of the coach, sirens wailing and a guy leaning out of the window signalling which way they're aiming. Madness.

You're headed for the Tattoo Club which, like all groooovy clubs in Rome, re-locates itself onto the beach in summer. At Tattoo, we're sitting in the open air like being trapped in a goldfish bowl under a palm leaf umbrella. Bright young things stand around in a circle and gape at this gilded elite. You can't do anything without one of our policemen escort friends asking to help. With Edge filming it on video camera, one guy leads you to the toilets, waving his torch to clear the route.

Bono's sneaking his way to the waves, followed by fellow-conspirators Eddie and Beth. "Where's Bono?" an Italian girl in an oo la la dress asks Eddie just as Bono purrs by her, and Eddie points back the way they've just come.

Soon all of us are sitting by the sea, Edge and Naomi and Christy having a bit of a splash of a paddle.

But now whizzing down the highway ... "I need a pee" says Naomi again. The coach can't stop, not right now anyway. Hard on our heels honking in crazed

jubilation are carloads of paparazzi bearing down on their prey. A paparazzi picie of Naomi pissing at the side of the road ... no way, José. Hard on the accelerator, baby. Think about **anything** but elephants. You tell Naomi that in the Apollo Theatre in the 60's when they had shows repeating all day long, they used to show a film of the Zambesi river during intermission, the idea being that all that moving water made people get up and take a leak ... and maybe leave so more punters could come in. Gotta pee. Naomi's saying how Adam's jealous that she met Bob Marley. Marley? Naomi would have been only a child. Which she was. She and a young boy were selected from their Streatham school to be in Bob Marley's video 'For Is This Love'. In the vid, you see Bob walking along holding the hands of the two children. "Actually, I fell asleep" Naomi grins, "and they kept it in".

Gotta pee.

The coach driver, he's doing his Le Mans trip shooting down the road like a, um, bat out of hell. The police car in front bounces just out of reach as it careers around the corners, tyres squealing and sirens screeching. We're in the middle of nowhere, kinda country vibes. Coach driver rattles to a halt, wheels locking onto gravel. Door opens, people pour out, those that have 'em with their appendages ready. The paparazzi who've managed to still tail us, their view is blocked off by the coach, David and Eric deliberately getting in the way of those intrepid and brazen enough to attempt to peer around our vehicle.

You stand there peeing in the soggy undergrowth that lines the road, the moon winking up above through the reeds and the bushes. There's a rustling sound beside you as the ground squelches and twigs break underneath somebody's feet. It's Bono balancing on the swampy ground as he shakes the drops off his one-eyed trouser snake. "Ah, showbiz ..." says the King B.

It's about 4.30 in the morning when we get back to the hotel. "I really fancy a pizza" Bono announces. "Anyone fancy a pizza?"

"Look, we're in Rome," Edge reminds his chum. "There's *no way* that anywhere will be open now. We're not in Dublin, y'know."

"If we *believe* we'll find somewhere open we *will* find somewhere open" you chirp up, the High Priest Of Happiness forever the optimist.

Bono climbs out of the coach to sign autographs for the fans waiting outside the hotel, then rejoins the depleted party in search of sustenance. Remaining in the huge cavernous coach are Bono, Eddie Vedder and Beth, Jeff Ament, King Boogaloo, Eric our security pal and the driver.

We squeeze down tiny streets, the driver like a camel herdsman carrying us through the eye of the needle. Finally we lose the remaining paparazzi and transfer to the limo that's been trailing us.

Paolo the limo driver searches Rome for our Holy Grail. He tries here, he tries there, checking the main avenues, driving carefully down ancient side streets where the buildings lean out almost converging above our heads. Our Paolo, he's a patient man. Mission Impossible seems to be the vibe. You remember as a child seeing a film where a little boy wants his sick donkey to be blessed by the local priest. *No way* is the reverend White Collar Worker going to bless *a bloody donkey*. Finally ... finally ... we see the determined little boy dragging his four-legged friend up the steps of St Peter's where Il Papa blesses his ailing pet. The donkey, natch, recovers miraculously. Don't give up was the message and it stood you in good stead ever since.

"Paolo," you say, "could we try *just one more* place, please?"

And there it is, a little hole-in-the-wall joint. It's

"UH...NO, WE'RE NOT A BAND"

empty and just about to close but the young Israeli who runs it, it's his birthday and he makes the strangers welcome. Il vino is now flowing and the Israeli's pal, he kindly hustles up pizzas from the tiny kitchen. Ah, nirvana!

The Israeli, he's a Led Zeppelin *fanatic*, pumping out the power of Jimmy and Robert and Jonesy and Bonzo from his tape deck. On the wall a picture of Robert, Viking ringlets cascading and a satisfied grin on his face, bears testimony to the fact that we're not the only rock'n'rollers to have discovered this culinary grotto. "Are you a band?" asks our host as the lead singer of U2 and Eddie and Jeff from Pearl Jam tuck into hot pizzas.

"Uh ... no, we're not a band" says Bono, honest as ever. You volunteer that you took some of the photos on Led Zep's 'Physical Graffiti' album, but our host figures you're fibbing. For once, actually, you aren't.

We leave, sated and grateful, to drop Eddie and Beth and Jeff off at their hotel, from whence they're leaving at six o'clock to fly to Ireland in a charter plane, to Dublin and then Slane Castle where they're playing with Neil Young and Van Morrison. "In Scandinavia," says Jeff, "Neil Young invited us to join him and his band which is Booker T And The MGs with Steve Cropper on guitar and Jim Keltner on drums, invited us to join him on stage

to play 'Rockin' In The Free World'. It was really *cool*." "That's one of the best things about what we do" adds Eddie. "We get to see some amazing bands ..."

As the limo purrs through sleepy Rome, it's getting bright now. We're passing the Victor Emmanuel monument ... no we're not. "Have we got time to get out?" queries Bono. Above us towers this classic building, a row of majestic pillars with atop 'em on each side four horses driven by a winged charioteer, built by Mussolini for his own glory.

Our bootheels echo in the dawn silence as we climb the steps to the right of the Victor Emmanuel monument and enter the square that was once surrounded by the old Roman parliament. Down another little laneway and now we're overlooking excavations. Below us, pillars rise up, pillars cracked by the scars of time.

Everywhere, it's quiet, very very quiet, a quiet broken only by the twitter of early birds who glide above us and our silent thoughts. No one says anything much. You, you're thinking about the pain it took to build these columns, slaves coming under the ruler's whip to create our private vision.

As we stand there, limo pilgrims carried back in time two thousand years, the lights of Rome are going out, extinguished one by one to meet the coming day.

November 21st 1992, Mexico City

Now you're in the front seat of a cab, going to Palacio De Los Desportes for tonight's gig with Rick Dobbis from Polygram and his girlfriend Marianne Koenig. Yo, B.A.D. II are going to be there too!

You're asking the cab driver how to say "It doesn't matter if you're gay" in Mexican, in preparation for when you do your verbal on stage about it all being love, "whether you're gay, straight, bisexual, trisexual". The cab driver's flummoxed.

"Maybe there isn't a Mexican word for gay" says Rick from the back seat. So how the heck are you going to say this to 20,000 Mexican U2 fans in a few hours?

"Okay, let me try this" you volunteer and now you're saying to the perplexed cabbie "It. Doesn't. Matter. If. You're. Not. Straight."

Ah yes, the driver gets it, he's rattling out his interpretation for you. You're slowing him down, writing it down phonetically and repeating his words to a look of growing and glowing consternation from his face. Rick and Marianne are roaring with laughter. "Am I that bad at it?" you say. "No", says Rick, "your pronunciation is very good. It's just that you're saying 'It's alright if you don't have an erection'!"

October 26th 1992, El Paso

In El Paso, this strange weird odd border town overlooking the poverty of Mexico, when you gaze out of your hotel window across the Rio Grande into the town of Juarez you can actually *see* where Mexico begins because the voltage on their electricity is less and thus the lights waft out a ghostly ghastly green hue ...

You go to an army surplus store to buy a $30 wooden US army trunk. You enter this emporium of American imperialism - "Bomb the bastards" and take the oil (and the cocaine to fund the CIA) seems to be the message - dressed like an African American freedom fighter in your Malcolm X jacket. Having spent less than $100 which includes the trunk, you exit in Desert Storm boots, Desert Storm trousers, Desert Storm shirt, Desert Storm jacket and Desert Storm hat and resemble nothing less than a skinny Stormin' Norman on Mexican mushrooms. Later, you discover that in El Paso there is actually, by some jest of nature, organic lithium in the water.

That explains *everything*.

BP: "It's alright if you

don't have an erection!"

November 9th 1992, Tijuana, Mexico

Bono's walking down a street in Tijuana and this street, it's like an open sewer and in the gutter there are food stalls. There are people cooking on trash can lids and as he passes one Bono reaches out and grabs what looks like a smoked ratburger and enthusiastically munches on it, followed by the music publisher Ken Friedman who, looking to the heavens, does the same.

Tijuana is strange because the U2 wanderers appear to be the only tourists in town. All the bars are open but there is no one in them except the unhappy workers and bar girls who used to be boys. Larry tries to take a leak in the street with a beer bottle in his hand - two different crimes - and when the police car turns up he attempts to run away. Suzanne drops her bottle of beer - another crime. The police frisk Larry and find his Swiss Army knife and this whole scenario is getting difficult, getting completely out of hand.

Paul McGuinness bounces into managerial mode, defusing the situation and negotiating carefully with the police and offering to be arrested as well. This noble gesture is made before he hears the stories of gringos being kidnapped by the Mexican cops. Paul is now proposing a solution. "Would you like some tickets for your friends for the show in San Diego tomorrow night?" The policeman, he's delighted at the suggestion. Suzanne springs into action. "Just you" Suzanne says, "just you plus one" as Paul is saying under his breath "Suzanne, get in the fucking bus" and Suzanne is saying "No, you plus one, that's all ..."

BP: "If you weren't in U2, Bono, what do you think you might be doing?" Bono: "I don't think there's anything else I can do. You see, in U2 I get to do everything I want to do - I get to make music, to play with video tape, to perform. Even the business end of things can be fun. We're in a corporation of five, there's a shit-load of dough that has to be dealt with and sorted out. I'm involved with putting that money to good use, But I'm also involved in spending that money on abuse" (laughs). "Y'know, just my own fun or whatever. I even get to wear a tuxedo for Frank Sinatra!" BP: "And what'll happen when the day comes, which it may or may not, when there is no U2?" Bono: "As soon as we feel we've reached a peak and we're repeating ourselves, that's when we'll knock it on the head. That will be our last album. What I'll do then I don't know. There's loads of things I love to do. I love to write ... prose, graffiti ... started a screenplay called 'The Million Dollar Hotel'. I've been asked to act in movies. We've taken on every other cliché and we might as well have a go at exploding that one ....."

BP: "Some bands go past their sell-by date. What d'you think, Edge?" Edge: "Thanx a lot, Beep! One of the good things about being in a rock'n'roll band, and a successful band, is that you don't have to think too far into the future, you can pretty much make it up as you go along. And that gives you control over your own destiny which is a very rare thing in the world today. We could break up, knock it on the head ... we could do another album, go on the road again, whatever. It's simply about the consensus of the four members of the group. So I don't know ... maybe we won't tour for another ten years. That's why I'm in a rock'n'roll band and not working in a bank. I like that freedom."

BP: "And if and when U2 comes to an end what do you hypothetically think you might be doing with yourself?" Adam: "Well, I don't know that U2 coming to an end would necessarily indicate that I was out of a job. I'm sure there would be other things going on, but it would depend ... I would have to see if I wanted to still be creative in a public way or whether I just wanted to be a little bit more private and do smaller things. I don't know how I'll feel at the time." BP: "But like what though? If you were to do smaller things?" Adam: "I've no idea how people survive so I'll have to learn."

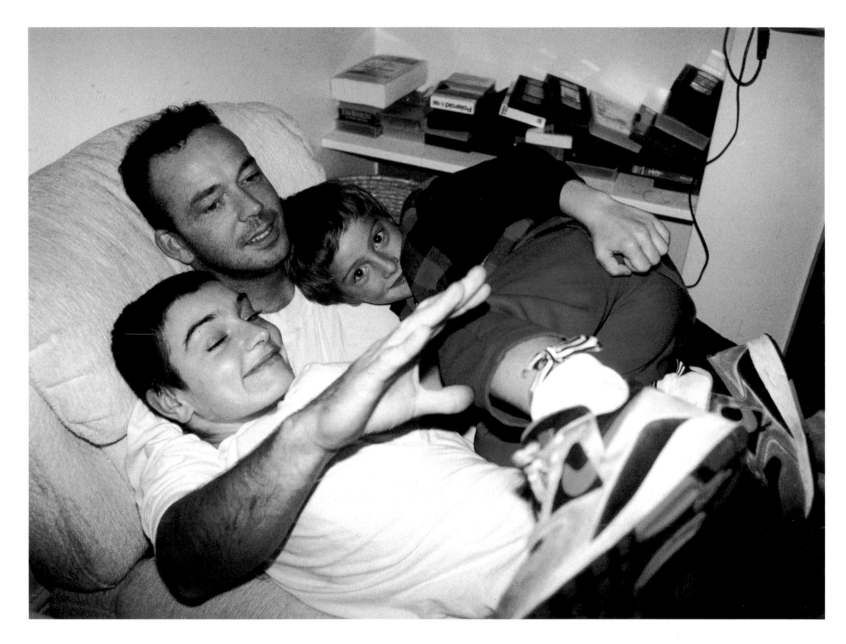

June 1st 1992, London

You're checking out and there in the lobby with the free strawberries Dennis comes up and says "What about this bill, then?" Dennis, he's holding a piece of paper. "This isn't your signature, is it?" No, no it isn't. It's a chit to your room for two bottles of champagne and a crate of beer. "What would you do if you weren't here with us?" Dennis says to you as he gently waves the document in front of a member of the hotel staff. You're thinking "Well I guess I'd have to pay it, wouldn't I?" and Dennis is saying "You wouldn't pay it, would you?" and then you're saying "No, I wouldn't pay it" and then Dennis is telling the hotel person it's nothing to do with you, someone's simply scribbled your name, someone who somehow knew your room number.

Several months later someone tells you, just out of the blue with no relationship to anything at all, the name of the person who scammed the champagne and beer. The hotel, y'dig, had only been serving residents. Big pressure, man. So this person had gone up to the bar and said "Well, I'm BP Fallon". Who? Gerry Conlon. Fair play, Gerry. Having been banged up for a lifetime I wouldn't have minded if you'd run off with the bed.

In The Name Of The Father

The Irish tourist in London in town for U2's Zooropa '93 Wembley Stadium gigs is staying at Sinéad's, her son Jake very kindly giving up his room for you. One night Jim Sheridan comes round and he shows a rough cut of his next film 'In The Name Of The Father'. Jim, he's shy about his new work, almost uncertain. The film, it's a tough and tender story about father and son, about British injustice, about being "Irish in the wrong place at the wrong time" as Shane MacGowan once wrote. It's about Gerry Conlon and the Guildford Four and it's about Gerry's relationship with his father Giuseppe.

Jim, he keeps asking "Do you think it works? Do you think people will be able to feel it?" Sinéad, she's gutted by Jim's film, completely moved. It is, actually, the work of a master.

Sunday you're down in Theale, Chris Blackwell's place in Berkshire. It's beautiful there, the Tudor black and white timbered house and the lake and going rowing in wild little round boats like barrels, paddling your own canoe with Chris there in the middle of the lake, his ever-ready mobile phone beside him.

Over dinner you tell Chris and Mary about seeing Jim's rough cut of 'In The Name Of The Father'. Chris says "Jim Sheridan is a genius". Apache Indian appears. Next thing you're in Ireland in Bono and Ali's drawing room, watching the latest cut of Jim's film with Chris and

Mary while Gavin and René pop their heads in and out.

Some days later Gavin says "I've written this song with Maurice The Man Seezer and Bono for the film, this song called 'You Made Me The Thief Of Your Heart' and I think it'd be brilliant to maybe ask Sinéad would she like to do it ..."

"Instead of checking into an asylum I've put myself into the studio with Gavin during the break after Zooropa and before we go to Australia and Japan" Bono announces.

Bono's saying that the song 'In The Name Of The Father' worked out really well. "Gavin does a Dublin talking rap in the middle which has lines like 'In the name

of freedom you drifted away ... in the name of United and the BBC, in the name of Georgie Best and LSD ...' It's kinda tripped out. And the song Sinéad sang, she sang it beautifully, one of the other two songs that Gavin, Maurice and I wrote, 'You Made Me The Thief Of Your Heart'." Bono's singing it to you now: "I hope you're happy now ... winter's cold but you're colder still, for the first time I feel you're mine ..." And now Bono's on the phone to home: "Who's silly? I'm your dad ....."

After the world premiere in Dublin of 'In The Name Of The Father' Gerry Conlon comes up to Bono, Gerry quoting Gavin's rap "in the name of Georgie Best and LSD!". Bono and Gerry are grinning. "You really got it right there" says Gerry.

Freezeframe: at STS Studios in Dublin, above the wonderful Claddagh Records record shop in Temple Bar ... Sinéad introducing her little doll to everyone as "Sinéad", singing like a Vedic angel, Gavin and Sinéad and Bono together finally in the studio after all these years.

October 1st 1993, The Clarence Hotel, Dublin

It's different now, different to the Dublin dawn over a year ago after the "Wise men say, only fools rush in ..." session at STS Studios, different now to when Bono, Gavin and King Boogaloo were knockin' at the locked 6 am Clarence Hotel door trying to get inside to get breakfast. Gracious, Bono - 'long with Edge and Adam and Larry and Harry Crosbie - they'd just bought the damn place and for Mr Fly the ex-Messiah it was definitely a Bethlehem vibe with "No brekkie here".

Now it's flashbulbs a go go, limos and bustle and blah blah blah.

Now it's - da da! - Gavin and René's wedding do, René radiant and shinin', Gavin in white suit, round black shoes, haircut just so, in the Tea Room of The Clarence Hotel.

Tom McGinty the Dice Man is MC, Gavin speechifying briefly like Oscar Wilde on a narrow sofa, the cigarette tracing patterns in the air as he addresses the throng, saying "I didn't have a best man but if I did it would be Bono" and Bono and the guys are grinning down at their pal from the balcony and one of Gavin and René's relations, one of the aunts unimpressed by this array of real live models of U2 she lets out the observation "Looka, there's your wan Naomi Campbell" and everyone roars with laughter, Naomi too. Perfect.

Once upon a time many many years ago before clouds ever cast a question mark across the moon and when the sun shone brightly every day there was in Lypton Village, this fantasmagorical place that lived in the minds of some young youths from Ballymun way, about 13 or 14 years old they were ... Among all the young dudes in Lypton Village, Gavin was 'In Charge Of Being In Charge' and Bono was 'The Judge'. Guggi, he was 'In Charge Of Stupidity' and Strongman 'In Charge Of Ignorance'. Bono into U2, Gavin, Guggi, Strongman, Edge's Dik into The Virgin Prunes. U2 to The Virgin Prunes were more like the, what, I don't know, The Beatles to The Rolling Stones' vulgarity and outrage. U2 and The Virgin Prunes with Gavin going on stage with a pig's head and in North Dublin's darkest alleys walking around in a dress and full make-up. Gavin, his real name is Finán Hanvey. 'Handbag Hanvey' they used to call him. By the time he gets to write the music for 'In The Name Of The Father', Jim Sheridan the film's producer is praiseworthingly describing Gavin as "an intellectual bootboy." Full circle. No pause button. October 1st 1993 at Gavin and René's wedding reception.

Downstairs in The Kitchen, the disco in U2's hotel, the unfinished disco still ready for its first hooley. Karaoke is the vibe in this crammed room, in-your-face karaoke with the performers only feet away. The lyrics travel the TV monitor as Ali, Siobhán Manuel, Christy Turlington and Naomi do their wild thing on 'Like A Virgin' all camp vamp, Anton Corbijn in his large cream suit entoning 'Suspicious Minds', Sheila Roche reprising her on-the-road restaurant and coach favourite 'Hey Big Spender'. Mr Pussy, Alan Amsby when life's not in drag, is lewder and ruder than Millie Jackson on a blue evening and he's hilarious.

The Dice Man is maestro, summoning victims from the floor. Reggie Manuel the Cocker Spaniel who's an optician has answered the summons for Reggie The Dog, the title he bore when he managed The Virgin Prunes. Reggie, he's metalling his way through 'Born To Be Wild'. The Dice Man calls out the name of Bono's father. Bono sitting on the steps beside you puts his hand over his face, whispers "Oh no, I hope he goes for it" and now Hewson Snr is happily singing Kris Kristofferson's 'For The Good Times', singing it flawlessly and graciously in the key in which he always sings it and it doesn't matter that the karaoke backing track is in another key entirely, doesn't matter a toss. It's wonderful, actually, Bono glowing and diggin' his dad. Edge has already put his heart into The Monkees' 'Daydream Believer', Guggi has emoted through 'Always On My Mind' and Gavin is now addressing his croon to 'Blue Moon', the words blipping up on the little screens. And now Gavin and Bono are on the tiny dance floor messin' it up like Bing Crosby and Frank Sinatra on a happy bender, mincing it out with "These boots are made for walking, and that's just what they'll do ..." and it's the ideal surreal cabaret.

And then Gavin, stripped of the karaoke backing track and without the words on the screen, alone with just his voice and his stagecraft, he performs 'Cabaret', every nuance, every exaggeration, every flash of warmth, every gesture loosely impeccable, "life is a cabaret, old chum, life is a cabaret ....."

Rewind: Bono and Adam and Edge behind Larry's right shoulder, the three heads leaning into their mike, doin' backing vocals. In front of them Larry in his jeans and leather waistcoat, shyness gone, relaxed, loose. Bono and Adam and Edge are chanting "the boys are back, the boys are back" as the lead vocalist Larry, he lets himself cook, his hand mike to his face, as he steams through Thin Lizzy's 'The Boys Are Back In Town', Larry out front, rockin', just doin' it, y'know, having a laugh, belting out "Guess who's just got back today, those wide-eyed boys that've been away ....."

Damn right.

THIS IS THE DIDLIOGRAPHY
"Nothing is real, nothing to get hung about." John Lennon
All photographs, unless otherwise credited, by BP Fallon. B/v = backing visuals

• Television Screen(s), The Globe, Stockholm, June 10th 92 • 2/3 Zurich, May 29th 92 • 4/5 Louisiana, April 2nd 92 • 6/7 Bono saluting: the Baltic Sea off Stockholm, June 9th 92; live Zoology - Bono: America, round two, 92; Edge: Paris 93; Adam + Larry: Europe 93 • 8/9 Times Square NYC, March 10th 92 • 10/11 Paul & Sheila: Zurich to Frankfurt, May 29th 92; Eileen & yer man: Hotel Majestic, Rome, am July 9th 93; Holly et al: MGM Grand, arriving Dublin Airport, April 92; Thingy & Regine: MGM Grand, Geneva to Bilbao, May 13th 92; Morleigh, Anne-Louise & Maurice: CNE Stadium, Toronto, am Sept 7th 92; Bono & Nassim: Juarez, Mexico, Oct 25th 92 • 12/13 Fintan: Aer Lingus, JFK to Dublin, am April 25th 92; Sheila, Dan & Keryn: going to the airport, America, round one, 92; Holly: Stockholm bay, June 9th 92; Suzanne: outside Ritz Carlton, Austin TX, 5th April 92; Sharon: Montreal, am April 28th 92; Ellen: Juarez, Mexico, am Oct 26th 92; Lyndsey & Dennis: Miami Beach FL, am Feb 28th 92 • 14/15 Outside Broadcast USA Tour programme 92 (design - Works Associates; photography - Anton Corbijn); BP: San Sebastian, May 13th 92 (photo - José Diaz & Monika Bilbao); Sinéad: Dublin 92 • 16/17 Factory rehearsals: Dublin, Feb 92; Ronnie & Edge: The Palace, Hollywood, Nov 18th 92; Ronnie: near The Pink Elephant, am Dublin 92 • 18/19 Flood & Bono: Ringsend Road, Dublin, April 93 • 20/21 BP & Bono (photo - Adam Clayton); Eno, Joe & Flood + Bono plugged: The Factory, Dublin, April 93 • 22/23 'The Wanderer' lyrics: Ringsend Road Studios, Dublin, April 93; Shoes + Apple: The Factory, Dublin, April 93 • 24/25 Albert King: Blues Etcetera, Chicago, March 29th 92; b/v Mike McCready & Dave Abbruzzese; Eddie, Mike, Edge, Christina & Jeff: The Metro, Chicago, March 29th 92 • 26/27 Edge serenity: Jimmy Carter Center for International Understanding, Atlanta GA, March 4th 92 • 28/29 Edge shopping: Little Five Points, Atlanta GA, 4th March 92 • 30/31 Edge spread, left hand column from top - Paris, June 27th 93; Gwenda & Garvin Evans & Dave Evans: MGM Grand, LA to Vancouver, Nov 2nd 92; Atlanta, March 4th 92; Stockholm, June 12th 92; Morleigh, Edge & Dik: Hippodrome de Vincennes, Paris, June 26th 93; right hand page, clockwise - Edge on TV: Pairc Ui Chaoimh, Cork, August 24th 93; MGM Grand, Kansas City to Denver, Oct 20th 92; Edge phone call: Outside Broadcast Tour USA 92; Edge laughing: Louisiana swamps, April 2nd 92 • 32/33 Louisiana swamps, April 2nd 92; Edge in BP's hotel room: The Ritz Carlton Buckhead, Atlanta, March 4th 92 • 34/35 Bono: Meat City NYC, am March 11th 92; meeting with Phil: The Hotel at Goodwin Square, Hartford CT, March 13th 92; JFK desk: Four Seasons Hotel, Boston, March 14th 92 • 36/37 One 'One' video shoot: Bono Vox + Edge & Adnana + Larry & Suzanne + Phil Joanou, Chris Blackwell & Paul + Edge, Adnana, BP & Queerdonna + mo' folk, Nell's NYC, March 11th 92 • 38/39 Mick Jones, Gary Stonedage & Chuck D: Legion Field, Birmingham AL, Oct 7th 92; Bono & Chuck D + Adam & Flavor Flav: El Paso to LA, Nov 92 • 40/41 Elvis shop: Manhattan, Aug 8th 92; Grey Ghost: Continental Bar, Austin TX, April 8th 92; Elvis still sleeping in Vegas, Nov 11th 92; Bono & BP: Palau Sant Jordi, Barcelona, May 16th 92 (photo - Stephane Sednaoui) • 42/43 Bono Vox + Bono twang + Bono & Gavin: STS Studios, Dublin, June 29th 92; Bono & Gav in the caff: off Capel Street, Dublin, June 30th 92 • 44/45 b/v: Elvis is still in the building; Gavin: St Stephen's Green to Lillie's, Dublin, am Aug 28th 93; Gavin shades: Harrisburg PA to Hershey PA, Aug 3rd 92 • 46/47 Crotch Music: The Forum, Milan, May 22nd 92; Vox Music: Westfallenhalle, Dortmund, Germany, June 4th 92 • 48/49 Bono watching playback of MTV awards 1992; Bobby & chums: outside Tivoli Theatre, Dublin, March 26th 94; Bobby + BP & Throb & Dizzy (photo - Alex Nightingale probably!): Dublin Stadium, March 25th 94 • 50/51 Ali & The Fly: Nassau Veterans Memorial Coliseum, Nassau NY, March 9th 92; Ali the day before Mr Pussy's opening night, Dublin, April 19th 94; Bob Hewson visiting, MGM Grand, 92 • 52/53 Bono & Edge: MGM Grand, JFK to Harrisburg PA, Aug 1st 92; Bono dressed up: Palace Of Auburn Hills MI, March 27th 92; Painting: Sinatra/model: Paul Hewson, at home, Ireland, Dec 27th 93 • 54/55 Valentino: Hotel Majestic ballroom, Rome, 8th July 93, on Kevin Davies photo shoot • 56/57 The Mirrorball Man: Palais des Omnisports de Paris, Bercy, May 7th 92; mo' Mirrorball: Ahoy Sportspaleis, Rotterdam, June 15th 92; The Flying Fly: Miami Airport, March 3rd 92 • 58/59 MacPhisto in St Peter's Square, Rome, July 9th 93, on Kevin Davies photo shoot • 60/61 MacPhisto ancora: Hotel Majestic, Rome, July 8th 93, on Kevin Davies photo shoot • 62/63 Left to right - Bono & new friends: Hershey PA, Aug 2nd 92; the S&M yoyo sequence: Florida rehearsals, Lakeland Civic Center FL, Feb 26th 92; mo' rehearsing: Florida, Feb 24th 92; Bono & still friends: as before • 64/65 Christina (anti-clockwise) - Zurichsee, May 28th 92; shimmering: St. Stephen's Green, Dublin, 92; twirling; airport flowers 92; Morleigh (left to right) - just out of reach + swirling + just out of reach: Zooropa 92; dressing room, Foxboro Stadium MA, am Aug 23rd 92; b/v Morleigh glowing • 66/67 Left hand page - BP & Michael: Ritz Carlton, Kansas City (photo - DeAnna Setzer); Bono beach baby, baby: Four Seasons Hotel, Boston, March 16th 92; Michael & Rono, Three Rivers Stadium, Pittsburgh PA, Aug 25th 92; Michael, Rono & Paul, MGM Grand, Detroit to Des Moines IA, Sept 11th 92; right hand page - Michael, Vaughn & Adam, Arrowhead Stadium, Kansas City IA, 18th Oct 92; Bono & Rono + Bono & Michael: MGM Grand, Detroit to Des Moines IA, Sept 11th 92; Edge, Michael & Vaughn: Boston, Aug 92; Mick Jones: going over the top of the Teotihuacan pyramid, Mexico, Nov 23rd 92; Michael: CNE Stadium, Toronto, Sept 5th 92; Gary Stonedage, Chris Kavanagh, Mick Jones & Nick Hawkins: Agora Ballroom, Dallas TX, Oct 15th 92 • 68/69 Mo Tucker: Baggot Inn, Dublin, Feb 13th 92; Deja VU: Mo' Mo, Bono, Sterling Morrison, John Cale & Lou Reed, • Strasbourg to Paris, am 24th June 93; Björk: the English bar, Las Vegas, Nov 11th 92; Bono, Benny & Björn + Benny & Björn again: Stockholm, June 10th 92 • 70/71 Mr Mirrorball: Tempe AZ, Oct 24th 92; Edge & Adam: The Dome, Tacoma WA, April 21st 92 • 72/73 Main shot - Son Of Sam II (photo - Bill Bernstein); outer shots (clockwise from top left) - space cadet, Oakland Stadium CA (photo - Laura Aryeh); all King Boogaloos: Yankee Stadium, NYC (photos - Bill Bernstein); Trabbie, Germany (photo - unknown); Boogaloo boots (photo - Gayle Mayron) • 74/75 Live & kickin': Zoo/Zooropa USA & Europe 92-93; Lou Reed: Stop Sellafield gig, Manchester G MEX, June 20th 92 • 76/77 b/v Heroes gig: SOBs NYC, before Fat Saturday 92; Bono The Drug Of The Nation: Pairc Ui Chaoimh, Cork, Aug 24th 93 • 78/79 GOD: America & Europe Zoo TV 92 • 80/81 Left hand page - Stephanie Seymour & Axl Rose: Dodger Stadium LA, Oct 31st 92; right hand page (left to right from top) - Dave Graham & Martin Gore: Palau Sant Jordi, Barcelona, May 18th 92; Bono & Winona: Four Seasons Hotel, Boston, March 14th 92; Heather Finley, Susie Q, Dr John & Donal Moylan: Tramps NYC, June 5th 93; mo' Mac & Willie DeVille: Galway Arts Festival, July 26th 92; Martika: Ritz Carlton, Central Park South NYC, am March 19th 92; Mr & Mrs Kevin Godley: Giants Stadium NJ, Aug 11th 92; Bono & Sugarlumps: El Paso to LA, Oct 27th 92; Björk & Einar Benediktsson: El Paso, Oct 26th 92; Sugarcube & Edge: El Paso to LA, Oct 27th 92; Bono & Peter Gabriel: Coliseum, Nassau NY, Mar 9th 92; Steve Jones: Dodger Stadium LA, Oct 31st 92; Björk & BP: Sun Bowl, El Paso, Oct 26th 92 (photo - Sugarcubes); Bono & Grace Jones: Marlin Hotel, South Beach Miami, March 1st 92; Axl & BP: Dodger Stadium LA, Oct 31st 92 (photo - Nigel Harrison) • 82/83 Paul & Dennis: Yankee Stadium NYC, Aug 29th 92; b/v Phil phoning • 84/85 High Priest Of Nonchalance, Miami Airport, March 3rd 92 (photo - Larry Mullen Jnr) • 86/87 Larry the Irish rover: Boston Gardens, St. Patrick's Day 92; Legs & Larry: BC Stadium, Vancouver, Nov 3rd 92; Bono & Larry: Mexican bus • 88/89 Gavin, Jaye Davidson & Boy George: Wembley Stadium, Aug 12th 93; Ali & Christy: Gavin and René's wedding, The Clarence Hotel, Dublin, Oct 1st 93; Boy George: Olympia Theatre, Dublin, Nov 27th 93 • 90/91 Bono on coach + Bono leaping: San Sebastian to Bilbao, May 15th 92; Planes & wheels: NYC, Miami & everywhere else; Bob Koch: MGM Grand, Kansas City to Denver, Oct 20th 92; Shanésia Davis: Ritz Carlton, Chicago, March 28th 92; Laura Aryeh: Mad Hatter's Hat Shop, East Village NYC, June 12th 93; BP's quarters, trying to escape, Four Seasons Hotel, Boston, March 18th 92 • 92/93 Bono & the burger: near Hershey PA, Aug 5th 92; Edge & Macca: BP's room, Harrisburg Hilton & Towers, Aug 3rd 92; Macca solo: shot out of window, Ritz Carlton, Sept 14th 92 • 94/95 Annie Leibovitz: Civic Center, Lakeland FL, Feb 29th 92; Danny: Ritz Carlton Buckhead, Atlanta GA, March 4th 92; Danny & Patsy: Mayfair Intercontinental, London, June 16th 92 • 96/97 The Wall Of Blame. Additional photographs by Patsy Dennehy, Saundra L. Schaffer, Larry Mullen Jnr, Barney by Hedge, Hedge by Barney, Stuart by Kirsten, Kirsten by Stuart, Bill Smythe (Vancouver presidency) & the Averill Archives • 98/99 Waterbaby + Paul + Suzanne & Bono & Paul + Nassim & Bono: Zurichsee, May 28th 92 • 100/101 Marley for ever, Kingston + CB at home on Strawberry Hill + grinnerama, St. Ann: Sept 26th to Oct 3rd 92; CB & Mary: Marlin Hotel, South Beach, Miami, June 93 • 102/103 Sinéad: elevator in the Rhiga Royal Hotel NYC, Oct 14th 92; Sinéad & Terry + Terry my friend: East Village NYC, Oct 14th 92 • 104/105 Edge before: Pairc Ui Chaoimh, Cork, Aug 24th 93; Edge after: RDS, Dublin,

Aug 28th 93; Robert Plant & the health freak: somewhere in Chicago, sometime in 1973 (photo - Cori Hinton) • 106/107 Daniel Lanois: Yankee Stadium NYC, Aug 29th 92; Daniel & Edge: Montreal to NYC, am Aug 28th 92 • 108/109 Shannon Strong (tape op on 'Achtung Baby' in Berlin) & the Duckwalker: Reeperbahn, Hamburg, am June 14th 92; b/v: For adults only • 110/111 El Beepo & Dawn: Joe King Carrasco's psychedelic bus, Austin TX, April 8th 92 (picie - JKC); Paul: Principle Management offices, Dublin, 1st July 92 • 112/113 Paul on the case: Brussels Airport, May 10th 92; Paul D-Day: MGM Grand, Kansas City to Denver, Oct 20th 92; Frank Barsalona, Paul, Barbara Skydel, Ina Meibach & CB: Palacio De Los Deportes, Mexico City, Nov 25th 92 • 114/115 Fiachna: Stansted Airport, July 3rd 92; hotel in Tallinn, July 4th 92; Boogaloo & Fiachna: Meadowlands NJ, March 18th 92; BG & Russian albums: Tallinn Airport, July 4th 92 • 116/117 JKC: Galveston Mardi Gras, Spring 93; Jerry Lee: Gaiety Theatre, Dublin, October 30th 93; Fiachna & Philip Dodd: Clarence Hotel, Dublin, 30th Oct 93; Fiachna, Jerry Lee & Katherine Fitzgerald: Gaiety Theatre, Dublin, October 30th 93; Rockin' Dopsie + David Rubin: Maple Leaf bar, N'Awlins, April 3rd 92 • 118/119 Edge & Adam, Mexico City nightclub, Nov 24th 92 • 120/121 Adam: MGM Grand, Vancouver to SF, am Nov 5th 92; Son Of Sam II: Yankee Stadium NYC, Aug 30th 92 (photo - Bill Bernstein); Adam & Edge also watching playback of MTV Awards 1992; Edge & Adam rehearsal: Sun Devil Stadium, Tempe AZ, Oct 24th 92 • 122/123 Salman Rushdie, Yasmin Le Bon nearly, Christy Turlington & Bono + Bob Geldof & Edge: RDS Dublin, am 29th August 93 • 124/125 Kraftwerk: Manchester G MEX Hall - Stop Sellafield gig, June 20th 92; Adam on beach + Help vibe: Sellafield, June 21st 92 • 126/127 B/v: the Holy Wall, Windmill Lane, Dublin, May 94; Sinéad: London, Aug 21st 93; Sinéad & Bono: Earl's Court Arena, London, May 31st 92; Sinéad & pals: Garden of Remembrance, Dublin, April 5th 93; jumping through the day: Windmill Lane, Dublin, April 2nd 93 • 128/129 U R here - buy this book • 130/131 Bono Voguing; Bono & red guitar & the truth, outside Harrisburg Hilton & Towers, am Aug 3rd 92; When Irish eyes are... • 132/133 Left hand page b/v - Yankee Stadium NYC, Aug 30th 92; right hand page (from top left to right) - TJ Thompson: Foxboro Stadium MA, am Aug 24th 92; riggers crewcut for Peter Kalopsidiotis by Warren Jones; Bono & Joe & Marian O'Herlihy: Danube Island, Vienna, May 23rd 92; Old Bill & Tim Lamb: Mile High Stadium, Denver CO, Oct 21st 92; Steve Iredale, Michael & The Duchess: backstage catering by Flying Saucers; Warren Jones tattoo & Paul; the Zoo Loo; MGM Grand visitation: Jake Kennedy, Peter 'Willie' Williams & Tim Buckley; Paul Oakenfold: Pairc Ui Chaoimh, Cork, Aug 24th 93; Trabbie painted by Cathy Owens: Hershey production rehearsals, Aug 2nd 92 • 134/135 Keef Riff Hard: The Academy NYC, am Jan 1st 93; Keef & Beep: mo' am; Eric Johnson & Jeff Ament + Eddie Vedder + Michael Stipe, Jane 'Sassy' Pratt & Neneh Cherry + Roisin Dunne, Jeff, Tom Morello, Michael & Neneh: Rock for Choice, The Palladium LA, Jan 23rd 93 • 136/137 The Bridge Club, Florida, am Oct 12th 92 • 138/139 Adam & cocktail dress: Don Cesar Beach Resort, St Petersburg FL, Oct 11th 92; Adam & Sebastian: Marlin Hotel, Miami Beach; Brian & Jo Clayton: Wembley Stadium, Aug 18th 93; Adam & Gail Elliot actually, near Rome, am July 8th 93; Arrested Development & Adam: MGM Grand, Detroit to Des Moines IA, Sept 11th 92 • 140/141 Adam & Naomi: Hippodrome de Vincennes, Paris, June 26th 93; Naomi: Hotel Majestic, Rome, July 8th 93; mo' Naomi in Rome • 142/143 Edge, Christy & Naomi + Bono & Eddie: Tattoo Club, somewhere near Rome, am July 8th 93 • 144/145 Christy & Edge in the goldfish bowl + Bono, Edge, Christy & Adam on the beach: Tattoo Club, Rome, am July 8th 93 • 146/147 Bono & Mickey Finn's: Hamburg, June 14th 92; Muleskinner Blues: Mexico, Nov 23rd 92; Bono carried away: Carlos'n'Charlie's, Mexico, Nov 23rd 92; Bono peeking on the Teotihuacan pyramid, Mexico, Nov 23rd 92 • 148/149 Outside Carlos'n'Charlie's, Mexico, Nov 23rd 92 • 150/151 County Wicklow, Ireland, May 1st 92; Bono resting: Ritz Carlton, Phoenix AZ, Oct 23rd 92; Paul & The Hype: Boston, am Aug 25th 92 • 152/153 Sinéad, John & Jake: London, Aug 13th 92; Jim Sheridan: at Mr Pussy's opening, Dublin, April 20th 94; Gavin & Bono: DNA Lounge, San Francisco, very am Nov 8th 92 • 154/155 'Bobby Hewson At The Sands' + the boys, back in town + Mr Pussy & Bono & Diceman plus one + Les Girls (Ali, Siobhán Manuel, Christy & Naomi) + Camp Gavin: Gavin and René's wedding, The Kitchen, Clarence Hotel, Dublin, am Oct 2nd 93 • 156/157 Bono: Meat City, am March 11th 92 • 158/159 This Is This Didliography: b/v Exile #9 by Boogaloo, Barney & Hedge, including 'Mexico' by Stephane Sednaoui • 160 Thanx & front cover: San Francisco Bay, Easter Sunday 92 • Back cover - BP: roof of the Marlin Hotel, South Miami, March 2nd 92 (photo - Anton Corbijn); Bono & les affiches: Lyon, May 12th 92; Edge: bound for Sellafield, am June 21st 92; Adam in Beep's drawing room: Sunset Marquis, West Hollywood, Nov 18th 92; Larry & Suzanne: one 'One' video, Nell's NYC, am March 12th 92 • Front flap - Bono & Edge: Palacio De Los Deportes, Mexico City, Nov 25th 92 • Back flap - BP laminate (photo - Holly Peters; accreditation - Suzanne Doyle); the Flying Works Associates: Shaughn McGrath, Steve Averill & Brian Williams, Works Associates, Dublin, April 1st 94. All captions approved by the FSC Committee 1994.
"Everything you know is wrong."

MO'OLOGY

"Contradiction is balance." BP Fallon

"Thank you for lettin' me be mice elf". Sly Stone immaculate again.

thanx

This book is dedicated with gratitude, respect and love to my parents, bless them, Colonel John and Kitty Fallon who allowed me to rock, and to my godson Danny Dennehy who allows me to roll.

And to Patricia Fallon. Patsy Dennehy. Susie Q.

Peter Fallon and Jean Barry and Adam and Alice.

..... and particularly to Joe King Carrasco, Noah and Dawn.

Annette Tallon. Valerie and Gerry Stevenson and Joy Denny and Mandrax and Emjie. Yo! Shirley Cullen, Martha and Louise at Switch.

Wim & Donata Wenders for lettin' me steal the title.

Bernard & Mary Loughlin, Maeve & Eoin, Teddy & Doreen Byrne, Regina Doyle and all at The Tyrone Guthrie Centre, Annaghmekerrig. Mo' yo!

With gratitude to Chris Blackwell & Mary & The Lunatic House JA too. Daniel Lanois & Jimmy Mac & The Magic House N'Awlins. Brian Eno & Flood. Much respect to Michael Franti & Ronno Tse & Vaughn & Merrie Martinian & Zulu from The Disposable Heroes Of Hiphoprisy. Chuck D & Flavor Flav & Public Enemy. Mick Jones & BAD II & BA. Sinéad O'Connor, Jake & John Reynolds. Björk & The Sugarcubes. Mo Tucker & The Velvet Underground. Bob Geldof & Paula Yates. Dave Stewart & Siobhan Fahey. Fiachna & Jadzia & Hothouse Flowers. Jerry Lee & Kerrie Lee Lewis. Rovena Cardiel. Laura Aryeh. Martha & Jessie Healey, Joanne & Glen Kernel. Eric Johnson & Steffa Smith, Eddie & Beth & Jeff Ament & Pearl Jam. Keef, Jane Rose, Phil Spector, Quentin Crisp, Shanésia Davis, Bobby Keyes. Adnana. DeAnna Setzer, Nigel Harrison, Michael Des Barres, Rookie, Clem Burke, Frank Infante & Dawn Loreen. Steve Jones. Axl Rose. John Sutton Smith. Yumi & Martin. Cori Hinton. Danielle Kraay. Bob & Christine Murphy. Paul Oakenfold. Jimmy & Percy & Jonesy. Bonzo. Benjie LeFeuvre & Rebecca. Elvis & Cait. Don & Linda. Joe & Marian O'Herlihy. Jake & Rocco. Pop & Mavis Staples. Grey Ghost. Lori Lightning & Sable Starr.

The Irish Arts Council and the Arts Council of Nothern Ireland. Keith Donald & The Arts Council Aer Lingus Travel Award Scheme & Dermot McLaughlin. Jack Van Zandt, Chris Charlesworth and Bill Huelster.

Xisle # 9 by Boogaloo, Barney & Hedge.

The Wall Of Blame by Boogaloo, Barney & Hedge & Nigel Harrison.

Tape unravelling by Stuart Smyth & Kirsten.

"Here we all are, sittin' in a rainbow" Steve Marriott & Ronnie Lane.

Dave & Ursula & Jack Fanning. Kirsty MacColl & Steve Lillywhite, Jamie & Louis. Gavin & René Friday. Majek Fashek. Dan and Orla and all The Hairboxes. Pat Burnett, Donal O'Malley & Catherine, Donal McNally. Gayle Mayron. Bill Kates. Yeah. Donal Moylan & Leslie Green, Saundra L Schaffer & Mark Slaughter. Paul Chicago. Salman Rushdie. Tone Löc. Ciaran Carty & The Sunday Tribune. Sandy Choron: keep on chooglin'! And Eileen Webster wherever you are/may be/will be.

Fachtna O'Ceallaigh ... love.

Dr Winston O'Boogie. The Fabs & Derek Taylor. Ronnie & Jo Wood, Leah, Tyrone, Jesse & Jamie. Seth Nettles, Henry McCullough & Josie, Marianne Faithfull. Agnes Burnelle. Steve Wickham & Anto Thistlethwaite. Johnny Angelo. Rasputin. Graham de Courcy Wheeler. Christy & Val Moore & Andy & Juno & Poraig. Nancy Moore. Ronnie & Deirdre Drew. Sharon Shannon. Frank & Ferga Murray. Martika. Ciara Cronin & Ciara O'Flanagan. The Pogues & Shane MacGowan & Joe Strummer & Joey Cashman. Rufus & Carla Thomas. Little Laura Dukes, Little Richard. Slash. Hedge & her funky fun-fur 4-wheeler.

Elvis, Marc, Jimi, Dr Winston O'Boogie again, Steve Marriott, Pam & Toby. Phil Lynott. Johnny Thunders. B12. Regine Moylett & Sharon Blankson. Neneh Cherry & Mother Moki. Bobby Gillespie & Robert Young, Primal Scream & Alex Nightingale & Murray Mitchell. Paul Wasserman & Brian O'Neill. Bo, Muddy, The Wolf, Sonny Boy, Willie Dixon, John Lee Hooker, Hubert Sumlin. Hank B. Marvin, Bill Monroe, Marilyn. Iggy & Suchi. Bob Marley, Hank Williams, Buddy Holly, Robert Johnson, Brian Jones, Ian Stewart. Roky Erickson, James Carr, Jim Dickenson, Peter Buck & Barrie. Fr Ronan Drury, Jnr Kimboro, Timothy Leary, Herb, a girl called Sandoz. The Fifth Letter.

And to you who knows my true name. Dedicated to everyone who came and to everyone who is still coming. God, Buddah, Allah and the whole gang: all the children boogie.

You. Me. Serendipity.

George Clinton, MLK, Malcom X, Nelson Mandella, Sly Stone. Paul Smith. Frank Paul. Rory Stokes. Technical Guru to King Boogaloo: Dave Evans.

Alan Duffy.

Philip Davies. Ray Flannery. Derek Swan. And Bob & Gretchen Koch.

Legal Stuff: James O'Malley & Lisa Johnston, Bridie, Terry & Yvonne NYC. John Doyle at Dillon Eustace Dublin.

Principle Management Dublin: Sandra Long, Candida Bottaci & ALK.

Principle Management New York: Ellen Darst still & Keryn Kaplin & Susie Smith.

Makin' movies: Ned O'Hanlon & Maurice Linnane.

On the road and onwards: Suzanne Doyle.

Paul & Kathy.

Larry, Adam, Edge & particularly Bono & Ali & Jordan & Eve.

Treble Yo! Philip K Dodd & Phil & Wan & the piano - blue pasta, respect & continuing enlarging thanx. Full moon over Sandycove ... and love, natch.

Rob Shreeve & Maggie for believing through the storms.

Carolyn Price for braving the storms and Michael Pietsch for rowing us to the promised land.

Right string baby and the right yo yo! Photographs: b/w printed by the virtually unreal Declan Barney Barnes at Kevin Dunne's Studio, Dublin. El mucho thanx, Barney. Colour by Neasa at The Colour Lab, Dublin. Thanx too to Lexington Lab NYC & Paris Photo Lab LA.

Mo' Yo Yo! Biggest shout out to Steve Averill The Designing Radiator, rapid singer of 'Television Screen' the year before he named U2, Brian Williams the Computer Suitor and Shaughn McGrath Superstath at Works Associates ... without whom. And Maria & Sarah & Maria ... without whom too.

Very, very, very, thank yis all .....

"Book after book, I get hooked every time the writer talks to me like a friend" Marc Bolan.

Bless us who are still alive and

bless us who are still in heaven. Amen.

BP June 1st 1994